D0094972

EUREKAAARGH!

EUREKAAARGH!

INVENTIONS THAT FAILED

ADAM HART-DAVIS

ACKNOWLEDGEMENTS

I am most grateful to Christine Foster, who spent many
hours poring over dusty volumes in the glorious dungeons
of the old Patent Office, and to Jolyon Troscianko, who
drew a number of the pictures.

Special edition for Past Times

First published in Great Britain in 1999 by
Michael O'Mara Books Limited
9 Lion Yard
Tremadoc Road
London SW4 7NQ

A CIP catalogue record for this book is available from the
British Library

1 3 5 7 9 10 8 6 4 2

Designed & Typeset by Design 23

Printed and bound by WSOY, Finland

PAST TIMES®

for Sue

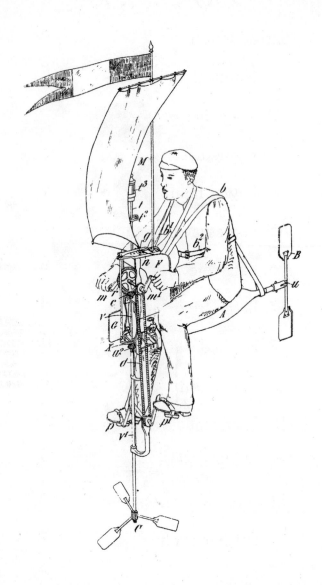

Contents

Introduction

In 1879 the Rev. George William Garrett designed, built, and launched the world's first powered submarine, which according to a newspaper report was 'very nearly successful'. Unfortunately, very nearly successful is not quite good enough, especially for a submarine, and that is what this book is about.

Inventions are often at the leading edge of technology; enthusiastic engineers believe that it must be possible to build a submarine, a human-powered aircraft or a beautiful new musical instrument. They patent the idea, go ahead and build it, and sometimes it works, but sometimes it doesn't. Good iron and steel became available in the middle of the nineteenth century, along with good steam engines to provide power; the urge to build machines must have been almost irresistible, and that must be one reason why the Victorians seem to have been especially ingenious and diverse in their ideas. Creative engineers in the middle of the nineteenth century must have felt that any sort of machine they could imagine must be not only possible to build but unshakeably successful.

When I started working on this book I was worried that it might be just a list of unlucky duds – and I kept feeling sorry for the person who invented the drink called 6-Up. However, the book seemed to take on a shape of its own, and I found that looking at the limits of possibility provided clues about why some inventions fell outside those limits. Sadly, I have only been able to scratch the surface of the subject; there are millions of failed inventions, and only a select few could get into a book of reasonable size.

I have generally avoided such pieces of technology as the telegraph or the Hansom cab, which were a great success in their day but have simply been superseded. Instead I have chosen particular areas of endeavour, such as flying and cycling, and within these areas have tried to show the great triumphs – the inventions that actually worked, alongside a number of near and not-so-near misses. As you will see, many of these 'failed' inventions were within inches of success – indeed, some did succeed briefly; the steam carriage is a case in point, for steam carriages ran on our roads for a hundred years. Others, however, now seem so far from the possibility of working as to be absurd. However, we have the benefit of hindsight – the only exact science.

Adam Hart-Davis
February 1999

1 Nautical nightmares

*Conquering the waves must have been a goal for
millions of people, from swimmers and canoe-paddlers
to those who designed the world's greatest ships. But
lurking for every swimmer and mariner are the desire
to go more quickly, and the possibility of disaster …*

Swimming machines

Liborio Pedrazzolli was born and raised in Italy and moved
to England about 1880. He married a local girl and set up a
business at 11 Hoxton Street, London, making and selling
mirrors, but he was also a keen swimmer.

I don't know whether he swam in the canal that runs
through Hoxton, or in a swimming bath, but he must have
been dissatisfied with the pull he was able to exert with his
hands, for in 1896 he took out a patent for swimming
umbrellas, to be held one in each hand, and the patent
explains clearly how they were meant to work:

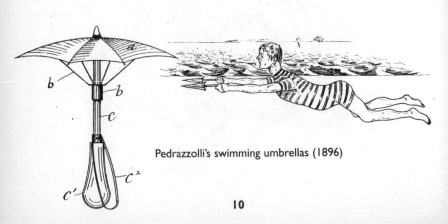

Pedrazzolli's swimming umbrellas (1896)

> **The apparati close when the hands are thrust
> forward thereby causing but little resistance or
> obstruction ... but when the return stroke is made
> the apparati expand in umbrella form, and the
> resistance thus offered enables the swimmer to pull
> or propel himself through the water at a speed
> hitherto impossible...**

These umbrellas are not a disaster. They do open and give
you a grip on the water. The problem is that they take about
one foot of travel to open – perhaps half a second. By this
time your hand is back level with your shoulder, and most of
the power of the stroke is gone – used up in opening the
umbrella. Meanwhile, every other movement is slightly
impeded by holding the umbrellas, so that, although they
probably speed you up a little at the end of the stroke, they
slow you down all the rest of the time. Maybe I just did not
make mine well enough. Perhaps you can do better.

More elaborate, and probably less efficient, is William A.
Richardson's Improved Swimming Device of 1880. According
to the inventor, transferring the work from the hands and
feet to the propeller enables the swimmer to proceed rapidly
and easily, at a speed of 4–6 m.p.h. Undaunted by this
invention, Gustav Zacher patented in 1899 a closely similar

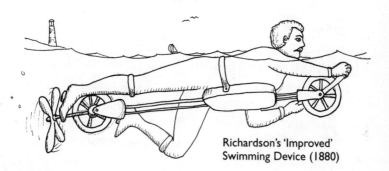

Richardson's 'Improved'
Swimming Device (1880)

machine with pedals for the feet to turn the propellers, and floats to take some of the weight of the apparatus. Mr Zacher claimed that the user could simultaneously swim and pedal:

> **Thus a peculiar double action is produced firstly by the swimmer moving himself forward directly and taking the apparatus with him, and secondly by the propellers driving the apparatus forward and the latter carrying the swimmer along with it. In the consequence of this double action and the essentially greater utilisation of the leg power the swimmer can travel in the water with the apparatus much more quickly than the ordinary free swimmer, or than a person on a water vehicle propelled by him by a treadling motion and screw propellers.**

It sounds to me as though Zacher expected his swimmer to be able to have his cake and eat it at the same time!

The problems I can see with this device are that carrying all that ironmongery about would make me sink instantly to the bottom; the thrashing of the elbows and knees would greatly impede progress; such propellers are hopelessly inefficient below speeds of about 200 r.p.m., which is much faster than the limbs can do under water; and finally, if it did get going, then the spinning of the propeller in one direction would tend to make the body spin in the other direction, which would be most disconcerting.

Life-saving equipment
Those who travelled by boat were always acutely conscious of the possibility of shipwreck, and many precautions were taken to prevent boats from sinking. Surrey engineer Fred Grantham Broughton patented a novel system of providing

Barathon Aîné's propeller-driven lifebuoy (1895)

the ship with a number of airtight tubes extending from the deck down through the bottom of the vessel, these tubes being closed at the top and open at the bottom, so that 'should the vessel, by reason of a leak, collision or any other cause, begin to settle in the water, the air enclosed … is gradually compressed by the water entering them, the contained air being ultimately compressed to such an extent that the pressure thereof counterbalances the tendency of the vessel to settle, thereby preventing its sinking.'

He also took the precaution of lining the ship with enough cork to keep it afloat even if it was riddled with holes.

The improved suit and fittings for 'Saving Life in Water' (1870)

There seem to be at least a couple of problems with this idea. First, filling the entire ship with air tubes and cork would leave no space for engines, cargo, crew or passengers. Second, he would do better to close his tubes at both ends, since the buoyancy of a parcel of air depends on its volume, and the compressing of the air would actually reduce the buoyancy, rather than increasing it as he supposed.

In general I think I'd rather stay in a regular vessel, but, just in case I do fall overboard, there is a splendid choice of lifebuoys. François Barathon Aîné of Paris patented a magnificent propeller-driven version in 1895 (see previous page). This provided the shipwrecked person with an inflated buoyancy bag to sit on, and had not just one but two propellers – one behind for cruising in search of help, and one below 'to prevent it sinking'. Both these propellers could be driven by pedals, by hand, or both. The shipwrecked mariner was provided with a compass, a small mast and sail, and a lantern to attract the attention of rescuers in the dark, plus 'a drawer enclosing toilet articles and boxes of preserved meat and fresh water'.

Even this luxurious device was a poor relation, however, of Captain John Benjamin Stoner's 'New or Improved Suit or Dress, and Fittings for Saving Life in Water', patented in 1870. The 'india-rubber suit of clothing made large enough to cover the person with all his clothing on', with the addition of an external jacket of cork, was designed to keep you afloat and warm, while 'a cap or hood is attached to the back and upper part of the said suit for covering the whole of the head and neck, except the face…' You were kept upright by lead weights fixed to the ankles. An attached floating hollow buoy provided flares, rockets, a flag for drawing attention to yourself and hand paddles for increasing your speed of swimming, while a floating accessory box contained drinking water, food, cigars, reading matter, a pipe and tobacco, so that when shipwrecked you could enjoy a good meal and a smoke, and read the news to pass the time before rescue – although how the newspapers were to be delivered is not quite clear; nor can I see how you could easily carry all this equipment with you at all times in case of the possibility of shipwreck!

Resurgam

In 1879 the Rev. George William Garrett designed, built and launched the world's first powered submarine, which according to a newspaper report was 'very nearly successful'. I was fascinated to discover the whole story.

George Garrett was born in Dublin and educated at Trinity College. He became a curate in Moss Side, Manchester, and later a commander in the Turkish Navy – but that's another tale. In 1878, while he was at Moss Side, he established the Garrett Submarine, Navigation, and Pneumatophore Company – 'pneumatophore' is a word usually used to describe the air bag jellyfish use for buoyancy – and in 1879 he designed his submarine ...

She was 45 feet (13.7 metres) long, and powered by steam. The boiler was stoked while she was on the surface, and then the fires were damped down and she submerged, using diving rudders. In theory she could stay under water for four hours, and do 10 miles (16 kilometres) at two or three knots. The Navy recognised her potential, and offered Garrett £60,000 if she passed marine trials in Portsmouth.

So he held a parish fête to raise funds, and launched her from Birkenhead. But she ran into a storm just a few miles into her journey; off Rhyl in North Wales the crew were taken off, and the submarine sank. She was called *Resurgam*, which is Latin for 'I will come up again', but unfortunately she never did.

However, the story is not yet over, for at the end of 1997 divers found *Resurgam*, a little rusty but in surprisingly good condition, on the sea bed off North Wales. There are speculative plans to recover her, and active discussion about how to preserve an ageing submarine.

The first submarine?

However, Garrett's was far from being the first submarine. The earliest we know about was apparently built about 1620 by the Dutchman Cornelis Drebbel, who was born in 1572 in Alkmaar, and moved to England at the request of James I. There is no clear contemporary description, but Drebbel's submarine was probably like two rowing boats, the second clamped upside down on top of the first, and the whole thing covered in greased leather. There was a watertight hatch, a rudder and four oars. Under the rowers' seats were large pigskin bladders, connected to the outside by pipes.

When the submarine set off, these bladders were empty

and tied shut with rope. When the crew wanted to dive they untied the rope, allowed the bladders to fill with water, and down she went. When they wanted to surface the crew squashed the bladders flat, squeezing the water out. This was enough to increase the buoyancy, and the vessel rose to the surface.

Drebbel was so satisfied with his submarine that he built two more, each bigger than the last. The final model had six oars on each side and could carry 16 passengers. The hull was strengthened with iron bands, and even had windows. This model was demonstrated to the King and thousands of Londoners. It could apparently stay submerged for three hours and had a range of six miles.

Allegedly the King declined the offer of a personal trip (sensible man!), but according to one account the submarine travelled in three hours the six miles from Westminster to Greenwich and back, cruising 15 feet (4.6 metres) below the surface. This seems unlikely: either the observer had a poor idea of time, or the submariners did not go all the way to Greenwich!

Since Drebbel built three submarines we can guess that they were rather more successful than Garrett's, but the idea of underwater travel does not seem to have resurfaced for a couple of hundred years.

The SS Bessemer

My favourite nautical nightmare was caused by the famous steel magnate, Sir Henry Bessemer. He was a self-made man who started from fairly humble beginnings, but managed to make a sequence of fortunes by putting bright ideas into practice. His first came from a process for producing bronze powder for making 'gold' paint. He discovered that the bronze powder cost seven shillings (35 pence) an ounce,

whereas the brass from
which it was made cost
only sixpence (2$\frac{1}{2}$ pence)
a pound – more than 200
times less – and he
realised there was an
opportunity to make a
financial killing.

He invented a set of
machines to grind brass
into powder, had separate
parts of the machines
made by various companies
all over the country,
assembled them himself in a
private house, kept each machine
covered in a separate locked room, and
then allowed no one inside the house except his brothers-in-
law for 35 years. So he kept the process secret, and without
ever taking out a patent made himself a fortune.

He invented a machine with heated rollers for embossing
patterns on velvet, a sugar-cane-crushing machine, and the
famous Bessemer converter, which allowed the finest steel to
be made some 5,000 times faster than had been possible
before. Indeed, it allowed mass production of steel for the
first time. In order to sell the process to the steelmakers of
Sheffield, he set up his own factory there, with offices in
Bessemer House, which is still there today, although the
factory has long gone.

On one memorable day Queen Victoria visited the
Bessemer plant. All the workers came in wearing their

smartest Sunday clothes. The Queen trotted in, safely enclosed in her coach, stopped for a few seconds without getting out, looked around with fascinated horror, and was then driven smartly out again.

Henry Bessemer had an idea for spinning artillery shells to make them more accurate. The British Army weren't interested; so he sold it to the French, which meant he had to cross the Channel frequently for consultations.

Unfortunately, Bessemer was a poor sailor, and was seasick on every trip. He wrote:

> **Few persons have suffered more severely than I have from sea-sickness, and on a return voyage from Calais to Dover in the year 1868, the illness commencing at sea continued with great severity during my journey by rail to London, and for twelve hours after my arrival there. My doctor saw with apprehension the state I was in. He remained with me throughout the whole night ...**

So, when he was financially secure, and his steel business was humming, he set about designing a boat in which he could not be seasick.

He approached this problem scientifically. Boats rock in two directions – they pitch from end to end, and they roll from side to side. The ship he designed was very long, so that she would not pitch, but rather sit across the waves. To eliminate the effect of rolling, he suspended the entire cabin on trunnions, with a huge weight underneath, so that, however much the ship rolled, the cabin would always stay level. In this way he hoped to avoid all the problems and to be able to cross the Channel in comfort.

He built a model of this ship, which was greeted with some scepticism, and then constructed a full-scale replica of

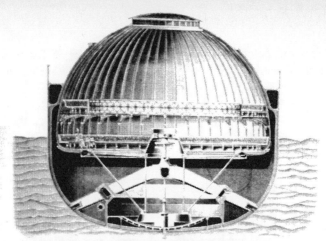

Anti-seasickness vessel: the SS *Bessemer* (1875) whose maiden voyage would be her last

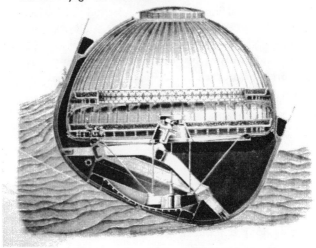

the cabin, 20 feet (6 metres) square and weighing several tons, in the field behind his house. It was made to roll through 30 degrees by a steam engine. This seemed to him to be a success, and, although others doubted whether the ship would work at sea, he went ahead and formed the

Bessemer Saloon Ship Company, and built the SS *Bessemer*. Her maiden voyage took place on 8 May 1875. She sailed majestically from Dover, on a fine calm day, crossed the Channel, and slowly but comprehensively demolished the pier at Calais. The SS *Bessemer* was completely impossible to steer, and she never put to sea again. The Bessemer Saloon Ship Company sank without trace.

Paddles and screws

A simple means of driving a boat is the paddle wheel driven by a bicycle mechanism, as used in an 1869 precursor of the pedalo. Paddle wheels were probably the earliest form of mechanical propulsion, and were employed in Mississippi river steamers in the early 1800s; steam engines to drive them were built and supplied by Matthew Murray in Leeds.

A rather more advanced piece of engineering is employed in Najork's foot-motor boat of 1895 (see over), which has a multi-rider bicycle superstructure, and is driven by a screw propeller. The invention of the screw propeller is a sorry tale. On 28 June 1834 the Rev. Edward Lyon Berthon, Rector of Romsey in Kent, was sketching the scenery as he travelled on a ferry on Lake Geneva, when a splash of water from one of the paddle wheels landed on his book, spoiling his sketch, and he thought instantly how stupid paddle wheels were. He reasoned that the whole propulsion unit should be under water, so that it couldn't splash.

When he returned to Britain the following year, Berthon set about solving the problem, and reckoned he could use a screw thread, rather like that on a woodscrew, only bigger, to allow the boat to pull itself through the water as a screw pulls itself through a piece of wood. He thought that he would need several turns to get a good grip of the water.

However, being a good scientist, he checked his theory

Ladies at leisure, men at work: Najork's foot-motor boat (1895)

by doing experiments. He dug a huge ring-shaped pond in his garden, and sailed a model boat around it, measuring its speed while it was propelled by various sorts of screw. Every time he shortened the screw, the boat went faster, until he ended up with not ten turns, not five, not even one, but with one-sixth of a turn. The rest of the screw, it turned out, was simply providing drag, and slowing the boat down.

Berthon called his invention the 'screw propeller', and took it to the Admiralty, suggesting they might be interested in developing it for the ships of the British Navy. However, the Admiralty mocked the idea, and said it 'was a pretty toy which never would and never could propel a ship'.

Berthon was so dispirited by this response that he gave up, but a few years later another man, Francis Smith, had the same idea, and after many years of argument he managed to get the screw propeller accepted. Eventually, the two men had the satisfaction of watching a naval review in which three hundred naval ships were all powered by screw propellers. Almost all ships use them today, and yet the screw propeller was originally turned down out of hand.

2 Tragedies of transport

Soon shall thy arm, unconquered steam, afar
Drag the slow barge, or drive the rapid car,
Or on wide-waving wings, expanded, bear
The flying chariot through the field of air.

ERASMUS DARWIN

Horse-drawn carriages

During the eighteenth century most people travelled by foot, although rich people had the option of riding on horseback or using a horse-drawn carriage. These varied from the lightweight racers to the great lumbering

Whoa! Annie Howell's 'Appliance for Stopping Runaway Horses' (1899)

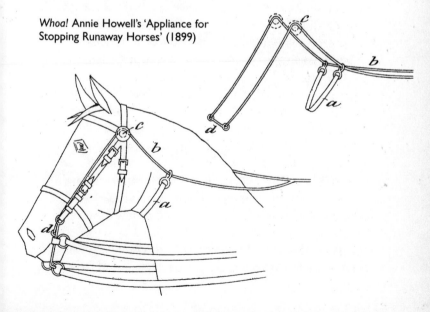

stagecoaches, but none travelled fast because the roads were so terrible.

Nevertheless, horses sometimes became scared, and bolted, and the runaway horse was a serious worry. Annie Howell from South Wales devised a way of stopping runaway horses by suspending a stiff strap between an extra pair of reins, so that when the reins were pulled the strap would press on the horse's wind-pipe, causing him to stop. This sounds rather unkind to me, and in any case it assumes that the driver will still be in position to grab the reins after the horse has bolted, which seems unlikely.

I prefer the hi-tech solution of John Young Walker MacAlister, who planned to mount an extra drum under the vehicle, driven by cogs or friction wheels from one of the axles. An extra pair of stopping reins was to be attached to the drum so that when the apparatus was brought into action the reins would be wound around the drum, pulling the horse's head back and forcing him to stop; the winding action would be released automatically when the horse's head was pulled well in. This still depended on the driver throwing a lever to put the apparatus into action, but presumably he could do this anyway if, for example, he had to get down to deliver something.

Some people designed their own carriages to suit their particular needs. Sir Joseph Banks – the rich fat botanist who sailed with Captain Cook on his first voyage around the world, enjoying a number of amorous encounters with the ladies of Tahiti, and was President of the Royal Society for 42 years – built a vast coach to carry him between his London house and his estate at Revesby in Lincolnshire. One of his long-suffering companions wrote:

> **It carried six inside passengers, with much more
> than their average luggage ... Sir Joseph ... travelled**

with trunks containing voluminous specimens of his *hortus siccus* in whitey-brown paper, and large receptacles for further vegetable matter, which he might accumulate in his locomotions. The vehicle had ... several fixed appertenances ... in particular there was a remarkably heavy safety-chain – a drag-chain upon a newly-constructed principle, to obviate the possibility of danger in going down hill, – it snapped, however, on our very first descent; whereby the carriage ran over the post-boy, who drove the wheelers, and the chain of safety very nearly crushed him to death. It boasted also ... a hippopedometer ... by which a traveller might ascertain the precise rate at which he was going ... this also broke, in the first ten miles of our journey: whereat the philosopher to whom it belonged was the only person who lost his philosophy.

Journeys with Sir Joseph were made even slower because every time he spotted a weed, or a tree with an unusual branch, he stopped the carriage and leapt out, armed with his magnifying glass and specimen jars, to botanise.

Erasmus Darwin, Charles's grandfather, was an enormously fat doctor who lived most of his life in Lichfield, Staffordshire, and needed his carriage to visit his patients in the surrounding countryside. He was immensely successful; on one occasion a man

Erasmus Darwin

came all the way from London to see him for a consultation. Afterwards, Darwin asked him why he had made the long journey, rather than visit the eminent Dr Warren in London. The man replied 'I *am* Dr Warren.'

Darwin was also popular and conscientious, and spent a lot of time on the road; so he made sure his carriage was convenient and comfortable. On one side of him he always carried a hamper of food in case he got hungry, along with a flagon of water, for Darwin did not drink alcohol. On his other side was a folding desk with books to read, and writing materials. He used to pass the time by writing poetry (see page 23), which was good enough to impress the poets Coleridge and Wordsworth, and was often concerned with matters scientific, since he was a founder member of the Lunar Society, and a close friend of James Watt and his colleagues.

Newcomen steam engines had been pumping water out of the mines for fifty years by then, and James Watt, prodded by the businessman and manufacturer Matthew Boulton, was talking of using steam engines to drive machinery; so the idea of steam-powered carriages was in the air. But the steam engines they knew were vast, heavy, lumbering beasts, firmly fixed in huge engine houses. To make a mobile steam engine needed new inspiration, and a new step in technology – high-pressure steam, which would deliver much more power for the weight of the engine.

Steam carriages

James Watt took out his famous patent for the steam engine with a separate condenser in 1769, although a further six years went by before he got the thing to work. In his wide-ranging patent, Watt suggested the use of high-pressure steam to push the piston through the cylinder. In practice he never used high-pressure steam – all Watt steam engines used steam at or below atmospheric pressure – but his patent was a considerable barrier to the use of high-pressure steam by anyone else.

Nevertheless, Erasmus Darwin was accurate in his prediction of steam-powered cars, or steam carriages as they came to be called. The first that we know of was built by the Frenchman Nicolas Cugnot in 1769, the same year that Watt got his patent. Cugnot's machine seems to have been a steam-powered gun carriage, and a picture of it is displayed on the monument in his home town of Void, in Lorraine. Apparently he made a model, and then constructed a full-size carriage, but it may never have been used. He seems to have used high-pressure steam, but to have underestimated the size of the boiler he would need to keep the engine going.

The second steam carriage was built by a brilliant Scot called William Murdoch, who was living in Redruth in Cornwall, where he was looking after the Boulton & Watt steam engines that were pumping water out of the Cornish mines. Like Cugnot, he realised that in order to get enough power from a steam engine he would need steam at high pressure, and in 1784 he built a beautiful table-top model some 18 inches (45 centimetres) long, complete with high-pressure steam engine and steering gear.

He was so pleased with this that he decided to go to London and get a patent; so he packed his engine in a box and set off with it in the coach. At Exeter the coach stopped to change horses, and he went for a cup of coffee, or maybe a pint, when whom should he meet but his boss Matthew Boulton, who was on his way down to Cornwall to see how Murdoch was getting on, and by pure chance had left Birmingham on the very day that Murdoch had left Redruth. Boulton asked where Murdoch was going, and when he heard the story he persuaded Murdoch that there was no future in patenting the steam carriage, and that Murdoch should return to Cornwall and get on with his job of maintaining Boulton & Watt engines. Matthew Boulton was merely being sensible in concentrating on their existing business; however, his intervention not only deprived Murdoch of some fame and fortune, but also deprived the world of the steam carriage for another 15 years, for they managed to get Watt's patent extended until 1800.

Luckily Murdoch had a young friend called Richard Trevithick, a fiery Cornish wrestler who enjoyed stamping the imprints of his opponents' boots on the ceiling of the pub in which they wrestled. Trevithick lived just down the road, having been born at Illogan. He was always an engineer at heart, and must have enjoyed watching the steam engines in the mines; no doubt he made friends with the resident Scottish engineer, and saw Murdoch's steam carriage.

Trevithick built his own high-pressure steam engines, and constructed a model steam carriage that he demonstrated on his kitchen table in 1799. By Christmas Eve 1801, when Watt's patent had run out, he had made a full-scale steam carriage – the Puffing Devil. On 28 December he set off for a test run. Unfortunately, after about a mile he hit a water gully, and turned the carriage over. The carriage was righted, but across the road Trevithick spied a pub. He went in for a drink to celebrate the first mile, then another … and another. They were still celebrating when the engine boiled dry and the road carriage exploded.

Not a man to be easily discouraged, Trevithick took out a patent for the high-pressure steam engine, and in 1803 went to Merthyr Tydfil in South Wales to sell some of his engines to Samuel Homfray, master of Penydaren Ironworks, where pig iron was made and transported down the valley to Cardiff. While he was in the Taff valley, Trevithick watched the horses pulling wagons of pig iron down the iron railway to the canal, and he reckoned that his engines could do the job instead. Homfray backed the idea. In fact, he was so convinced it would work that he wagered another of the mine captains, Anthony Hill, 500 guineas (£525) that Trevithick's locomotive would haul 10 tons of iron from his Penydaren works to Abercynon Wharf and pull the empties back, by steam power.

Now Trevithick had to make his dream work, and the day of the great trial was set for 21 February 1804. Trevithick's locomotive was hitched to five wagons carrying 10 tons of pig iron and 70 passengers, including Anthony Hill. They had some problems: the chimney was too high to go under overhanging branches; so they had to cut down a few trees on the way. But they made it – the locomotive hauled its load the full 10 miles of track in a speedy four hours and five minutes, making an average of a little over 2 m.p.h.

That was the world's first train journey! You can still see the remains of the track where the journey took place, along the old tramway that is now the Taff Trail cycle track. The grooves in the stones where the rails used to lie are clearly visible.

The reason that Hill was so confident in waging 500 guineas and declaring the journey impossible was that no one believed you could get enough friction between the wheels and the rails to pull the load of a train. Trevithick's solution was weight: he built his engine up to 5 tons, which meant he had plenty of traction on the rails, especially as he had to haul the load downhill to Abercynon.

However, the track had been built for horses rather than 5-ton engines, and many of the cast-iron tram plates were broken by the massive beast. Trevithick had to drive it back on the road. As a result the wager was declared void, and, more important, Trevithick's locomotive didn't catch on. Homfray and other mine owners were not prepared to replace their tram tracks with stronger ones suitable for steam locomotives. That did not become economic until the cost of horse fodder mounted a few years later during the Napoleonic Wars. By then, Trevithick was in South America seeking his fortune, but some young engineers in the north were happy to make locomotives for the new tracks. Their names were Matthew Murray and George Stephenson.

Trevithick had shown that mobile steam engines could deliver enough power to drive carriages, and various people went on to develop the idea, no one more enthusiastically than another Cornishman, Goldsworthy Gurney.

Gurney was born on 14 February 1793 at Padstow, had a medical practice before he was 20, married a farmer's daughter the next year, moved to London in 1820, and in 1823 won the Gold Isis medal of the Royal Society for his oxyhydrogen blowpipe. Having seen Trevithick experimenting with a steam engine on wheels while on holiday at Camborne in 1804, he patented a steam carriage in 1825, and in 1826 he founded the Gurney Steam Carriage Company (GSCC) and began manufacture. At first he put the boiler under the passenger seats, but realised this might inspire terror, and in 1828 designed and built a Drag, which was a separate engine to pull the coach, rather like a railway

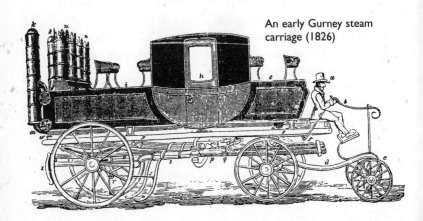

An early Gurney steam carriage (1826)

locomotive pulling passenger coaches.

In 1829 he was invited by the Quartermaster-General of the Army to make a trial journey to Bath and back. They set off at dead of night on 27 July from Cranford Bridge Inn on the Bath Road, which is roughly where Heathrow is now. Gurney and two engineers rode on the Drag, towing a carriage carrying Gurney's brother Thomas, one of the GSCC's directors, Colonel Viney, and Captain Dobyn. There was also a horse-drawn phaeton and a post-chaise with extra supplies of coke.

At Longford they collided with the Bristol Mail on a bridge, and broke one of the driving irons; they had to carry on the best they could with steam power being supplied to only one wheel; and they had to push the carriage up hills. They went through Marlborough and Devizes to Melksham, where they arrived about 8 p.m., and at a fair in the marketplace were attacked by a crowd shouting 'Down with machinery. Knock it to pieces!' Gurney was cut on the head.

They had four days' rest in Bath, and then drove back to London. For the whole trip they averaged 15 m.p.h., which was much faster than the mail coach. Indeed this was the first long journey at a maintained speed by any mechanised vehicle. Two weeks later, on 12 August (when he might have been shooting grouse), the Prime Minister, the Duke of Wellington, asked for a demonstration in Hounslow Barracks, where the Drag pulled the Duke's carriage around the yard, and later a wagon carrying 27 soldiers.

These demonstrations showed that the steam carriage presented a commercial opportunity, and in 1831 Sir Charles Dance started a regular steam carriage service from Cheltenham to Gloucester – nine miles, four times a day. This ran for five months, but was then sabotaged by the mail-coach owners.

Steam carriages might have become a major force in mechanised transport, but their future was cut short first by the sabotage and second by a short-sighted government. Unfortunately the government decided that the railways, which by the early 1830s were being built in the north and planned in the southwest, were the best thing for the country; so they not only backed the railways with an Exchequer Loan of £100,000, but also rushed through a series of Turnpike Bills which put prohibitive tolls on horseless carriages. Gurney had to abandon the whole enterprise in 1832, and lost £232,000. However, a plaque in the church at Poughill, on the edge of Bude, says of Gurney:

> **His inventions and discoveries in steam and electricity rendered transport by land and sea so rapid that it became necessary for all England to keep uniform clock time.**

Steam-carriage enthusiast John Scott Russell

There were a few other steam-carriage disasters. After some consultation with Gurney, John Scott Russell, the man who later built I.K. Brunel's biggest ship, the *Great Eastern*, started his engineering life by persuading some Edinburgh businessmen to set up the Scottish Steam Carriage Company. The tolls were prohibitive for the road between Edinburgh and Glasgow, but they carried 26 passengers on an hourly service between Glasgow and Paisley, running at an average speed of 14 m.p.h., until, on 29 July 1834, one of the wheels collapsed, possibly as a result of sabotage. The furnace and boiler ruptured with a mighty roar and a gush of steam and cinders, and four passengers died.

The Earl of Rosse, President of the Royal Society and builder of the world's largest telescope at Birr Castle in the middle of Ireland, had a rather wild family. His son, Charles Parsons, invented the steam turbine, which now provides power in most power stations, but when Charles was a lad he and his brothers built their own steam carriage to get around the Birr Castle estate, and had the misfortune to kill a favourite aunt in an accident when the carriage tipped over.

Atmospheric and pneumatic railways

One of the main reasons for the decline and eventual failure of the steam carriage was the arrival of the railways, which by the 1840s were snaking their way across Britain. However, their motive power was not always a picture of success.

One of the most spectacular failures of judgement shown by the larger-than-life engineer Isambard Kingdom Brunel was over the South Devon Railway (SDR). He had already built the Great Western Railway (GWR), with its impressive broad gauge, which reached Bristol in 1841, and had then extended it to Exeter. When he became engineer for the SDR in 1844 he surveyed and planned the most spectacular route. As soon as the rails had cleared the city of

Renowned engineer Isambard Kingdom Brunel: however, his atmospheric railway hopes never got off the ground

Exeter they were to leave the land altogether.

The railway would follow the Exe estuary to Dawlish Warren, curl round the coast to Teignmouth and up the Teign estuary to Newton Abbot, and for maximum effect Brunel wanted to build this entire 20-mile section on stilts, a hundred yards offshore. The people of Dawlish protested vigorously that the railway would destroy the prospects of their important holiday resort, and reluctantly he agreed to put his line on dry land. However, it still runs all the way along the very edge, within yards of the waves.

Furthermore, he persuaded the company that he should use the newfangled atmospheric propulsion system, which he claimed would not only be more economic but would also provide more power when the trains needed it to get up the serious inclines along the southern edge of Dartmoor, especially at Rattery.

An atmospheric railway was far from a new idea: in the late eighteenth century an atmospheric train had been proposed that would run entirely within a cast-iron tube, propelled along it by air pressure, but nothing was built at the time. However, in the 1830s several new systems emerged, of which the most promising was developed by the Samuda brothers in Croydon.

This used normal rails, and between them was a cast-iron tube, 9 inches in diameter. A piston ran along inside the tube, and was connected to the leading passenger car. The air was pumped out of the tube in front of the train to create a vacuum; so the piston was pushed along by the pressure of the atmosphere behind it, and the piston pulled the train. It was indeed an atmospheric railway.

The Samuda brothers demonstrated the system to all the leading railway engineers. George and Robert Stephenson would have none of it, but Brunel was fascinated, and with his brilliant salesmanship he persuaded the directors of the

South Devon Railway to approve it. This was to be the first major railway designed from the start to be atmospheric.

Brunel chose 15 inches (37 centimetres) for the diameter of his pipe along the coast, and planned to increase it to 22 inches for maximum power inland. The vacuum was created by huge Boulton & Watt steam engines set in pumping houses every three miles along the track. The plan was that when the train reached a station they would telegraph ahead to the next pumping house and tell them to switch on the pumps and make a vacuum ahead of the train. When all the passengers were aboard, the brakes would be released and the train would glide silently forward. Because the trains didn't need locomotives they were much lighter, and so the rails themselves were lighter and cheaper.

The first atmospheric trains ran from Exeter in March 1847; the first timetabled passenger service operated from 13 September, and by February 1848 the whole 20-mile run from Exeter to Newton Abbot was atmospheric.

The passengers loved the atmospheric system. The trains ran quietly, and without steam, smoke or smuts. What's more, the atmospheric trains had tremendous acceleration and deceleration. On one epic test run outside Dublin, a young man called Frank Ebrington got into the front carriage, didn't realise the others had not been coupled to it, and was hauled along a mile and a quarter of sharply curving track at a terrifying average speed of 84 miles an hour. For the 1840s he was certainly the fastest man on Earth!

The South Devon trains normally did 40 or 50 m.p.h., and they were often on time or even ahead; one train ran from Newton Abbot to Exeter in 20 minutes, which is faster than today's Intercity trains.

However, there were technical problems. Casting the pipe was difficult; eventually Tom Guppy in Bristol managed to turn it out at the rate of a mile a week. Even more of a problem was the valve along the top. The pipe had a three-inch-wide slot all the way along the top to allow the connection between the piston and the carriage. The slot was closed in front of the train by a flap of leather with an iron frame that fitted into the slot to maintain the vacuum.

Unfortunately this leather flap sometimes froze solid in the winter, and dried out in the summer sun, so that getting a good vacuum was difficult. Greasers were employed to walk along the track smearing the leather with mixtures of lime soap and cod oil, seal oil or whale oil. Unfortunately the oil attracted rats, and the rats ate the leather – and that didn't do the vacuum any good either.

The organisation needed to set up the system efficiently was sadly lacking. The pumping engines turned up on time, but sat in the rain for many months before the pumping houses were built. The pipe was delivered on time, but had to wait around for a year while the track was laid. Worse, the leather seal lay around too, and may well have deteriorated beyond use before it was even installed. The telegraph instruments were never put in place.

Getting the pumps to work properly proved hard. There were no filters; so when they were switched on in the morning each pumping station was like the inside of a vacuum-cleaner bag. With the first rush of air came a mixture of oily water, rust and dead rats and mice. Because the telegraph never worked, and the leather seal leaked, the pumps had to operate all the time to maintain a useful vacuum, and this was very expensive.

There were other problems too. Atmospheric trains could not reverse; so it was embarrassing if they overran the platforms by even a few yards – the passengers had to get out and push – and shunting around stations was impossible. What is more, no one ever solved the problem of points – one track could not meet another, because there was no way of getting the rolling stock across the cast-iron tube between the tracks.

Brunel was hopelessly busy at the time. The *Great Britain* was being fitted out and launched – and then ran aground; he was in charge of the Clifton Suspension Bridge, Sunderland Docks, Bristol Docks, the Merthyr & Cardiff Railway, the Cheltenham Railway, the Bristol & Exeter and so on; it seems to me that he never really concentrated on the South Devon Railway.

In 1844 railway fever was at its height, and Brunel persuaded the board to go atmospheric with a flurry of magnetic personality and the promise of cheaper running, backed up by rather dubious economics. By 1848 the tide had turned. The atmospheric system was out of fashion, and by a bit of sharp accounting the anti-atmospheric lobby managed to persuade the shareholders the railway had made a loss in the first six months of the year. This was unheard of – no railway company had ever made a loss.

In fact they were owed a load of money for carrying mail, and the company was moving sharply into substantial profit, but the fudged accounts were enough; the atmospheric system was abandoned. The last atmospheric train arrived at Exeter in the early hours of Sunday, 10 September 1848, and the system closed down for ever.

However, Brunel's embarrassing disaster did not prevent others from developing the idea in different directions. In 1853 Latimer Clark started dispatching messages through long tubes $1\frac{1}{2}$ inches in diameter between the Central and Stock Exchange Stations of the Electric and International Telegraph Company in London, a distance of 220 yards (200 metres). The carriers fitted like pistons, and were pushed through the tube by atmospheric pressure after a partial vacuum was created at the receiving end.

In the late 1850s this pneumatic dispatch was extended by laying down radial pipes, along which the carriers containing Post Office telegrams were dispatched outward by positive air pressure and back in by vacuum. The pipes, which generally became standardised at $2\frac{1}{4}$ inches diameter, were first made of iron, and later of iron lined with lead, with soldered joints, which gave a smooth internal surface. They were up to half a mile long, and the felt-covered gutta-percha carriers, with up to 12 telegrams held in by a rubber band, travelled 1,000 yards (914 metres) in a minute. So successful was the method that by 1885 London boasted a total of 82 tubes, covering a total range of 33 miles, and there were similar operations in Liverpool, Dublin, Manchester, Glasgow, Birmingham and Newcastle, as well as in large cities on the mainland of Europe. A similar communication system was often used in offices and hotels, and also in shops for conveying money to the cash desk and returning the change.

Encouraged, no doubt, by the early success of this pneumatic dispatch, entrepreneurs tried carrying people in the same way – in a coach that just fitted inside the tunnel, and was propelled along it with a blast of compressed air. At Crystal Palace gardens, in Sydenham, south of London, T.W. Rammell opened, in 1864, a pneumatic railway with a

tunnel 10 feet in diameter; it ran every afternoon, and for a fare of sixpence ($2\frac{1}{2}$ pence) would carry passengers for a third of a mile across the gardens. The passenger car had a capacity of 85 people, and was propelled by the compressed air from a large fan driven by a steam engine.

New York's first subway car (1870)

Much cheered by these British experiments, Alfred Ely Beach, at one time owner of the *New York Sun* and *Scientific American*, built a model pneumatic railway for the American Institute Fair in New York in 1867. It carried passengers just 35 yards from 14th Street to 15th Street, but it was a tremendous success. During the exhibition it carried 170,000 passengers, and won Beach a gold medal. He went on to dig a 100-yard tunnel underneath Broadway, cunningly evading the attempts of the hostile mayor to block his progress. The whole tunnel was dug in two months.

On 28 February 1870 the tunnel was officially opened, to dazzling effect. The *New York Times* reported:

> **Certainly the most novel, if not the most successful, enterprise that New York has seen for many a day is the pneumatic tunnel under Broadway ... Yesterday the tunnel was thrown open to the inspection of visitors for the first time and it must be said that every one of them came away surprised and gratified.**

The *Evening Mail* said:

> **Even as we write, a comfortable passenger car is running smoothly and safely between Warren and Murray streets ...**

The passenger car used in the tunnel was circular in cross-section, richly upholstered and very comfortable, with seats for 22 people, and it was propelled by the compressed air from a 100-horsepower steam engine. Meanwhile the waiting room boasted frescoes, chandeliers, a fountain, a grand piano and a grandfather clock! Unfortunately Beach's attempts to extend the system were blocked, at first politically and later economically, and he died in 1896 without having managed to build any more.

3 Flying fiascos

The first successful balloon flight was achieved by the Montgolfier brothers in 1783, and balloons filled with hot air, hydrogen or helium have been flying about ever since. More recently they have been joined by their more sophisticated siblings, airships. However, balloons and airships can carry only small payloads, or a few people, and they are rather at the mercy of the wind. As a result, people have for hundreds of years tried to follow the birds, by building heavier-than-air flying machines.

Early dreams

Daedalus and his son Icarus, according to the Greek legend, tried to escape from captivity on the island of Crete by flying like birds. They made themselves wings by using wax to stick feathers to their arms, and flew off the island, but Icarus was enjoying the sensation so much he became foolhardy, and flew too high – too close to the sun. The sun's heat melted the wax and he crashed to his death in the sea. According to some modern ideas, Daedalus, who was a canny engineer and the architect not only of the labyrinth but also of King Minos's fabulous palace at Knossos, had invented the hang-glider.

People must always have wanted to fly. Birds look so wonderful as they soar overhead, and watching seagulls and rooks you can easily believe that flying would be easy and fun. Leonardo da Vinci clearly thought so. His notebooks

This inventor may well have spent too long with his head in the clouds

contain detailed sketches of birds in flight under various conditions of wind and weather, and of a number of flying machines, powered by hands or feet. None of these was technically possible around 1500, but Leonardo did not let impracticality stand in the way of his imagination.

What is slightly surprising, however, is his optimism. He fully appreciated the size of birds' wings and muscles in relation to the rest of their bodies, and yet he sketched human-powered flying machines with wings too small to support human weight and yet too big to be driven by puny human muscles.

Batty bedstead-flying machine as dreamt up by Dr W.O. Ayres (1885)

Flights of fancy did not end with Daedalus and Leonardo. How about the wonderful vehicle dreamed up in 1885 by an American doctor, W.O. Ayres of New Haven? Ayres must have been impressed if not mesmerised by the power of compressed air. His flying bedstead was to be held up like a helicopter by four propellers mounted on vertical shafts and powered by turbines, driven by compressed air stored in two cylinders. The aeronaut was to sit on a bicycle saddle, control the supply of air with his left hand, and propel the machine forward by driving a horizontally mounted propeller with his right hand. Meanwhile, with his legs he would pedal to assist the lifting rotors. Luckily for the aeronaut, there can have been little danger of this machine leaving the ground!

Sir George Cayley

Over the centuries, hundreds or even thousands of people must have tried to imitate the action of birds, making artificial wings and trying to glide or flap through the air. The first serious attempts at aerodynamic experiments were made in the 1790s by Sir George Cayley at his home Brompton Hall, near Scarborough in Yorkshire.

The balloon was invented when George was nine years old, and he became fascinated by the possibilities of flight. He spent hours studying the flight of crows; he measured the rate at which they flapped their wings, and reckoned they had a wing area of about a square foot (0.09 square metres); so when he began tests he too used a square foot of wing.

Any sort of aerodynamic testing in the open air is plagued by variations in wind speed, not to mention rain, damp and sunshine; so he moved indoors, and built a whirling-arm machine to investigate lift well away from the wind and weather. According to legend he waited until his wife had gone off to stay with her mother for the birth of their first child, and then quickly installed his whirling-arm machine in the stairwell of the hall.

He used a falling weight on a string wound round a vertical shaft to spin a horizontal arm, like a broomstick, on the end of which he mounted a square foot of wing for testing. This meant the test wing was always being pulled by the same force, and always through nearly still air. He quickly found that with a flat wing the amount of lift depended on the angle between the wing and the horizontal – the angle of attack. A horizontal wing produced no lift at all, while a wing angled up at 45 degrees gave a good deal of lift, but also whirled rather slowly, because it generated a lot of drag. What he needed was the optimum compromise of maximum lift with minimum drag, and his results suggested that the best angle of attack for the wing was 6 degrees, which he used on the aircraft he later built.

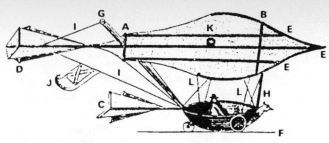

Cayley's designs for a flying-machine (built 1853). His research made big advances in the theory of flight

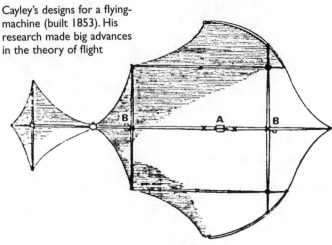

Cayley seems to have been the first person to realise that in order to fly you need both lift and forward propulsion, and that these two things are quite separate. Birds like seagulls can glide for hours without flapping their wings; they must still be able to get lift while they are gliding. So it cannot be necessary to flap your wings just to stay up; therefore he began to design aircraft with fixed wings. He seems to have flown his first model glider in the early 1800s, but he was a busy MP and landowner, and did not get around to building a full-sized aircraft until 1853. By then he was 79, and rather old to learn to fly; so he volunteered his coachman John Appleby to be the world's first test pilot.

The aircraft was taken to one side of Brompton Dale, a narrow valley opposite the house, and hauled across the grass by half a dozen farmhands pulling on ropes. It took off and flew across to the other side of the Dale – a distance of perhaps 200 yards (180 metres) – and crash-landed on the grass just before the trees. This was almost certainly the world's first flight by a man in a heavier-than-air machine. Appleby crawled from the wreckage and said, 'Sir George, I wish to give notice; I was hired to drive, not to fly!'

Cayley reckoned that gliders would be much better than mules for bringing people, especially injured people, down from the Alps, and he waxed eloquent about the future of air transport; he wrote of the air as a second navigable ocean that extends to everyone's front door. He produced several papers about aeronautics and aircraft design during the first half of the nineteenth century, and the Wright brothers gratefully acknowledged his work after their tremendous success at Kitty Hawk in 1903. Cayley never seriously attempted powered flight, although he did experiment with a gunpowder engine, and he predicted that no one would achieve powered flight until he could get 100 horsepower into a pint pot.

John Stringfellow

However, the first powered flight had already been achieved five years before Cayley's coachman's epic flight, in the summer of 1848. John Stringfellow, another Yorkshireman, had first caught the flying bug from one Samuel Henson, with whom he went into partnership for a time. Cayley had studied crows; Henson and Stringfellow studied rooks, and reckoned they carried about half a pound (0.23 kilo) of weight on a square foot (0.09 square metres) of wing; their aircraft were designed with the same sort of ratio of wing area to weight. But Henson was enormously ambitious: he not only tried to build flying machines but also tried to set

A replica of Stringfellow's (1848) model: the first powered aircraft, but a steam engine would never carry a man to the skies

up an airline. Ridiculed by the newspapers and magazines of the day, whose artists let their imaginations loose on the absurd idea of carrying passengers in flying machines, Henson finally gave up his flying ideas, patented a new safety razor, and moved to New York.

John Stringfellow, left to carry on alone, built a model aircraft to his own design in Chard in Somerset, powered it with a tiny lightweight steam engine, and flew it inside the top floor of a lace mill. The aircraft was only a model with a ten-foot (3 metre) wing span, and it flew only about ten yards (9 metres), but there is no doubt that John Stringfellow was the man who first achieved powered flight.

Bird-men
During the second half of the nineteenth century, dozens of intrepid Victorian would-be aviators invented a great array of weird and wonderful flying machines that had about as much chance of flying as lead balloons with heavy anchors

in tow. Perhaps they never saw pictures of the Cayley and Stringfellow machines, or perhaps they just ignored all the work that had been done and ploughed their own furrows – literally, in many cases!

One of the most curious of these machines was a 'natural flying machine' proposed by an American in 1865. He had clearly thought about the effort exerted by birds, and wrote from Baltimore suggesting that since a brown eagle can carry off a baby or a lamb, weighing perhaps 20 pounds (9 kilos), then 10 eagles should be able to carry an adult human. He suggested that the eagles should have fitted jackets which would be attached to a circular framework of hollow tubes which in turn would carry a

A seriously bird-brained idea: one inventor's dream of flight (1865)

basket, rather like the baskets carried by balloons. He imagined a network of cords passing through the tubes, which would allow the passenger to control the altitude of the machine by compressing or releasing the birds' wings, and a similar system to control direction by swivelling the birds' necks to point the right way. He does not mention such problems as how to persuade the birds to fly at all, nor how to prevent them from plunging to earth if they spied a tempting rabbit or other form of lunch.

Mr W.P. Quimby of Wilmington came up in 1871 with a system so elementary that it is scarcely any advance on the wings of Daedalus and Icarus, except that the wannabe flyer is supposed to be able to help flap by using his leg muscles, since a piece of rope is tied from each ankle to the corresponding elbow. This must be a good idea in principle, since the leg muscles are much bigger and stronger than those in the arms and shoulders, but my instinct is that the long piece of rope between the wing and the ankle would be more likely to cause some unpleasant dislocation of the hip or one of the leg joints than to allow any useful extra effort to be used for flight. What's more, Quimby's wings must be too small.

Could people fly?

Henson and Stringfellow calculated that a square foot of wing could support half a pound. Let us suppose for a moment that this is about right. Then to support the weight of a light intrepid aviator of say 150 pounds (68 kilos) – just less than 11 stone – the wings would need an area of 300 square feet (28 square metres). Mr Quimby's wings have an area of about 30 square feet (2.8 square metres), which is 10 times too small.

Consider the muscles too. An Olympic gymnast can just support himself for a few seconds by his hands on the rings

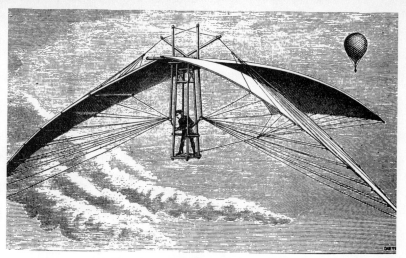
Over in a flap: de Groof's fatal flying-machine (1874)

with his arms straight out sideways. Most of us would be quite unable to do this, and yet to fly upward with a wing on each arm would require greater strength than simply to hang motionless. Therefore our arm muscles are nowhere near strong enough to fly with. We can walk upstairs, and even run upstairs for short periods, but to climb, say, 100 feet (30 metres) in a minute is a major effort even for the powerful leg muscles. So, if a human being is to fly using muscle power, the legs should do most of the work, and the flight can only be slow.

An ingenious and amazingly brave Belgian inventor, Mr de Groof, spent years designing and building what he called a parachute, to imitate the action of birds. His framework was made of wood and rattan and covered with strong waterproof silk. His wingspan was nearly 40 feet (12 metres), and the total area of the wings and the tail must have been close to 300 square feet (28 square metres); so at least he was in the right ballpark. He controlled the machine by three hand-operated levers.

For his first trial, he jumped from a great height on to the Grand-Place in Brussels, which was a complete flop, but luckily he escaped unhurt. He then went to London, where a balloonist, Mr Simmonds, took him in his machine to a height of 450 feet (137 metres) and then released him. I am amazed. However confident I was in my theory of flying, I should not be keen, after a crash, to start my second test flight from 450 feet (137 metres) above anything, let alone London! However, de Groof glided safely down and landed in Epping Forest. But on 9 July 1874 he tried again, with fatal results. Mr Simmonds took him up to 1,000 feet (300 metres) and released him, and de Groof's plan was to glide down and land in the Thames. Alas, however, on release the wing frame collapsed, and the courageous de Groof plunged to his death.

One of the most sensible of the human-bird inventions was the flying apparatus of the German Otto Lilienthal. Following in Cayley's footsteps, or rather glidepath, he studied the flight of birds, and wrote a book about it as a basis for the art of aviation. His apparatus was astonishingly similar to the modern hang-glider, although he had to make the wings of thin osier rods covered with fine linen. In flight they became slightly concave underneath, like the wings of a heron – or a hang-glider. He also fitted a prominent tail fin in order to steer, and reported that on a high, long-distance flight he succeeded in making a turn of 180 degrees, so that he ended up flying in the opposite direction.

At first he jumped with his wings from a high tower on a hill near Berlin, which must have been awkward, but then he moved to a 200-foot-high hill in the Rhinow Mountains near Neustadt. Of the moment when he first unfolded his wings on the hill, Lilienthal said:

> I was overcome by anxiety at the thought that I was
> to descend from this height into the wide expanse of
> landscape which stretched out far beneath me. But
> the first cautious attempts at diving soon restored
> me to the consciousness of safety, for I took off
> much more gently from here than from the tower
> which was my former launching-point.

He also described vividly the method and sensations of
flying:

> With folded wings you run against the wind and off
> the mountains, at the appropriate moment turning the
> bearing surface of the wings slightly upward so that it
> is almost horizontal. Now, hovering in the wind, you
> try to put the apparatus into such a position in relation
> to the centre of gravity that it shoots rapidly away and
> drops as little as possible. The essential thing is the
> proper regulation of the centre of gravity; he who will
> fly must be just as much the master of this as a cyclist
> is of his balance. Obviously, when one is in the air
> there is not much time to ponder about whether the
> position of the wings is correct; their adjustment is
> entirely a matter of practice and experience. After a
> few leaps one gradually begins to feel that one is a
> master of the situation … the aviator … travels over
> deep chasms and soars for several hundred yards
> without the slightest danger, parrying the wind
> successfully at every moment.

Unfortunately, on 9 August 1896, Otto Lilienthal was testing
a new type of steering device, crashed to earth from a height

A hell of a ride:
Goupil's flying
machine (1885)

of 50 feet (15 metres), and broke his spine; he died the next day. His last words were said to be 'Sacrifices must be made.'

One idea that definitely escaped de Groof was that there was little point in trying to flap – Cayley had shown that it was not necessary – and therefore there was no point in having two separate wings, since the 'shoulder joints' would come under tremendous stress; much better to rely on a single strong spar from wing tip to wing tip, with no hinge in the middle. Lilienthal's hang-glider may or may not have had such a spar. He talked of his 'wings', but they may have been rigidly fixed together.

The machines of de Groof and Lilienthal were gliders, and not only did they have a reasonable chance of success, having roughly the right area of wing and not expecting too much of the pilot, they both worked to some extent, and their inventors definitely enjoyed real flight. When it came to powered machines, however, many inventors seemed to take leave of their senses, or at least made absurd assumptions about the strength of human muscles.

In 1889 John P. Holmes of Oak Valley, Kansas, dreamed up 'a light and strong machine for navigating the air, designed to be readily controlled by the aeronaut to give the best possible results in flight with the least expenditure of power'. The pilot lay on his stomach on a canvas support, steering with his feet, controlling the pitch – that is the angle – of the aeroplane with one hand, and using the other to turn the curious propeller in front. 'The aeroplane is arranged to be rocked up and down, and locked at any desired adjustment, for utilising wind currents and the propelling force of the wind to the best advantage.'

Not only is the wing – perhaps 30 square feet (2.8 square metres) including the tail – far too small to support a human being, but the idea of using only one hand for propulsion is ridiculous: imagine trying to swim using only one hand to pull yourself forward – trying to do pull-ups or climb a rope to beat the pull of gravity.

Mr A. Goupil's aeroplane of 1885 had slightly more chance of getting off the ground, although I would not be keen to put money on it. The wing area is only about 50 square feet (4.6 square metres) (wooden strips covered with silk), but at least Mr Goupil planned to use the leg muscles for power. Cunningly, as the pilot pedals furiously, he turns both the wheel between his feet and the propeller in the nose. Thus, 'as the apparatus obtains velocity its weight diminishes on account of the increase of the vertical reaction of current, and, finally, it ought to ascend and maintain itself aloft ...'

Pedalling for the sky (1888). I doubt it!

although in practice I doubt whether it actually did so.

The 1888 pedal-powered helicopter is another optimistic device. Here there is nothing fancy – merely a minimal frame and a large rotor, powered directly by the pedals. Even if the rotor could be 100 per cent efficient, however, trying to lift yourself like this would be like running upstairs at full speed carrying the helicopter, which would need a pilot of exceptional power and stamina. An additional problem is that because of Newton's third law of action and reaction, when the rotor turned anticlockwise the rest of the machine would necessarily spin clockwise, which would be most disturbing, and would probably, within seconds, make the pilot violently airsick.

Theodore A. Stark of Ottawa, Illinois, designed in 1893 a motor turned by both hands and feet:

> **thus enabling every muscle in the body to be used to supply the driving power for, say, a flying machine. The flyer lies in a framework of tubes, his feet hook into movable rods, his arms move a second set of rods, and all these movements are transmitted to an endless belt which runs over two pulleys. The motive power is then transmitted from there to the propellers.**

All I can say is good luck, Ted Stark! The wing area is perhaps 100 square feet (9 square metres) – so he isn't going to stay up for long. And all those rods and belts and pulleys are going to use up at least half his energy in overcoming friction. I should expect his maiden flight to be mainly downward – and terminal.

So, in their fantasies, the Victorian inventors came close to the modern hang-glider, but they were a long way from achieving human-powered flight, which did not happen until 23 August 1977, when a superfit cyclist and hang-glider expert, Bryan Allen, pedalled his way into the air and round a figure-of-eight course around two markers 800 metres apart, as prescribed, in order to win the Kremer Prize of £50,000.

The aircraft in which he achieved this amazing feat was the *Gossamer Condor*, designed by the aeronautical engineer Dr Paul MacCready. Built from balsawood, cardboard, superthin Mylar plastic film and piano wire, the *Gossamer Condor* weighed only 70 pounds (32 kilos), and yet had a wingspan of 96 feet (30 metres). Since the total weight of the pilot plus the plane must have been between 200 and 250 pounds (90–113 kilos), the wing area of some 500 square feet (46 square metres) was just about in line with the 1840 calculations of Henson and Stringfellow. The pilot steered with his hands and pedalled furiously to turn the propeller using his leg muscles to get lift and propulsion.

The following year Allen flew a slightly more advanced aircraft, the *Gossamer Albatross*, across the English Channel, taking nearly three hours, fighting a headwind, to cover the 23 miles. Since then there have been a number of other human-powered flights, including one of 70 miles, which took four hours.

Engine-powered aircraft

John Stringfellow just managed to achieve flight using a steam engine, but his was an ultra-lightweight steam engine, and his aircraft never took off from the ground: he launched it from a wire. The mill in which it flew is some 25 yards (23 metres) long. He slung a wire from one end to the middle, sloping slightly down, so that once the engine started the aircraft would accelerate down the wire and then launch itself with a simple mechanical trip when it came to the end. In this way he could be sure it would be travelling at flying speed when it first went into free flight, and also travelling dead straight and level, since the aircraft had no tail fin for lateral stability, and the wing tips had only about five feet (1.5 metres) of clearance on each side.

The experiences of Cayley and Stringfellow seem to have passed by Joseph Kaufmann of Glasgow, who in 1869 designed a steam-powered aircraft in the form of a bumblebee. The 40-horsepower steam engine weighed 2.5 tonnes – it would have made a good steam carriage or small railway locomotive. To get this into the air he attached a pair of wings, each 35 feet (10.6 metres) long, which the engine was supposed to flap 120 times a minute. To ensure the stability of the aircraft in flight he suspended a 90-pound (41-kilo) weight underneath, on a long telescopic rod.

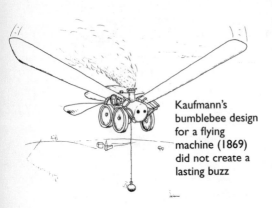

Kaufmann's bumblebee design for a flying machine (1869) did not create a lasting buzz

Let's just consider the facts. The wing area, assuming the wings were to be 6 feet (2 metres) wide, would have been about 420 square feet (39 square metres), which when gliding would be enough to carry 210 pounds (95 kilos) – but the steam engine weighed 25 times that! No chance of gliding, then. Meanwhile if the wings flapped through an arc of 30 degrees – which is modest, since the wings of most birds and insects flap through at least 90 degrees – the wing tips would have to travel at 200 feet (61 metres) per second, or 150 m.p.h. Even worse, they would have to go backward and forward three times a second, reaching this speed on

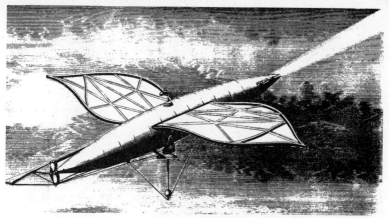

Professor Baranowski's 'gigantic bird' (1883) was another flight of fancy

each stroke. There is no material capable of taking such stresses – the wings would break apart in seconds.

Undeterred by such considerations, however, Kaufmann planned a machine with a 120-horsepower engine, which he claimed would be able to carry three gondolas with a few passengers at 56 m.p.h., with fuel for 10 hours and water for three. However, his 40-pound (18-kilo) model, supplied with steam from an outside source, was not a great success. During a demonstration the wings did indeed make flapping movements, but when the steam pressure was increased the wings finally broke, and the model was seriously damaged.

Joseph Kaufmann was not the only one. The Russian Professor Baranowski designed a more futuristic but equally implausible steam-powered aircraft, and apparently demonstrated a model of it at St Petersburg in 1883 (a small model without a steam engine, I suspect!). The cylindrical machine was to take the form of a gigantic bird. The task of the powerful steam engine inside was not only to flap the wings but also to drive the three propellers – one in the stern and one under each wing.

Maxim's maximum flight was only a second or two (1894)

Steering was to be achieved by means of oarlike rudders, one each side of the tail. The 'beak' of the bird was to have an opening to allow the ingress of air for the crew to breathe and the fuel to burn, while the escaping smoke and steam would make the huge craft resemble a comet with a luminous tail. And once again there was to be a weight suspended below the machine to keep it properly in balance.

On 31 July 1894, according to *Scientific American*, 'for the first time in the history of the world, a flying machine actually left the ground, fully equipped with engines, boiler, fuel, water, and a crew of three persons.' Unfortunately the proud inventor, Hiram Maxim (famous for his machine gun), 'scarcely had time to realise his triumph before fate, which so persistently dogs the footsteps of inventors, interposed to dash his hopes.'

The Maxim flying machine was a vast structure of steel tubes and wires, with a maximum of five pairs of wings and a wingspan of 125 feet (38 metres). The crew stood on the deck at the bottom, along with the boiler and gasoline. The twin 150-horsepower steam engines, mounted 10 feet (3 metres) above the deck, each drove a propeller nearly 18 feet (5.5 metres) across. A reporter from the *Pall Mall Budget* described vividly the scene when both engines were running:

> **The platform on which we stood rocked and quivered with the vibration. A hurricane seemed to spring up, laying the hay flat far and wide, and scattering like a whirlwind the shavings in the workshop 20 yards away. Every one grabbed his hat with one hand, and clung for dear life with the other to the rail.**
>
> **Suddenly, when the tornado had reached its height, and the whole machine was shaking and straining at its anchor like a greyhound in the leash, a shrill whistle gave the order to 'let go', and the huge structure bounded forward across the meadows with a smooth sailing motion, at a rate increasing up to 40 miles per hour.**

However, although this vast machine flew for a second or two, it crashed back to earth, embedding its wheels in the soft grass, and 'in a moment it lay stretched on the grass, like a wounded bird with torn plumage and broken wings.'

The steam engine, as Cayley and Stringfellow had realised, could never deliver enough power for an effective flying machine; that had to wait until the turn of the century, when the internal-combustion engine became readily available; then the aviator could indeed get 100 horsepower into a pint pot, as Cayley had dreamed.

4 Power failures

*The simplest form of power is muscle power. For
thousands of years people farmed their land using their
own effort and that of their horses, mules, oxen or
bullocks. Then, often within the organisation provided by
monasteries or by the army, engineers began to harness
such natural resources as the wind and flowing water.*

Blowing in the wind

Windmills were allegedly invented in the Middle East,
although probably they and water wheels were dreamed up
in various parts of the world. One of the more elegant
windmill designs was patented by Benjamin Wiseman Jnr, a
merchant of Diss, Norfolk, in 1783. The beauty of this
construction was that the direction of the wind did not
matter: it would still revolve, like four boats sailing in a
circle. The problem was that each sail had to go about and
gybe on every revolution, and repeated gybing in a strong
wind will tear any sail to pieces; it can even break the mast.

In 1828 the citizens of Bristol were astonished to see a
new vehicle, pulled by a kite, sailing along the roads, over
the downs, and into the hills. 'After many experiments Mr
George Pocock,' according to the *Annals of Bristol*, 'invented a
vehicle somewhat similar in form to the modern tricycle,
and found that one of these, capable of carrying four
persons, could be drawn by two kites of twelve feet and ten
feet in height respectively – the speed attained with a brisk
wind being about twenty-five miles an hour.' He called his

kite-powered carriage a charvolant, and demonstrated one to George IV at Ascot races in 1828.

The *Liverpool Mercury* recorded that Pocock used kites to pull a ferryboat across the Mersey, and said that with the largest kites and a good wind, a boat 'would be able to make the passage from and to Birkenhead, whatever might be the state and strength of the tide', and that the boat could be drawn in any direction 'less than five points from the wind'.

According to Pocock's *Treatise on the Aeropleustic Art, or Navigation in the Air, by means of Kites or buoyant sails, with a description of the Charvolant, or Kite Carriage*:

> Mile after mile, in succession, has been performed at the rate of twenty miles an hour, timing it by chronometer in hand. A mile has frequently been performed, over a heavy road, in two minutes and three quarters. Let it be noticed, that the wind was not furious, neither were the kites additionally powerful for the bad state of the roads ...
>
> That the swiftness of movement should almost prevent breathing, is certain, if going against the wind; but when travelling at such a rate, it is with the wind, and thus a perfect calm is enjoyed. One evil, however, it was supposed did arise from its velocity – loss of appetite; for on one occasion, when pulling up at a house of call seventeen miles from Bristol, some little concern was felt by the party when not one of them was disposed to take any refreshment. ... However ... on looking at the chronometer, they discovered that their travelling pace, up hill and down, had been sixteen miles within the hour: of course there could be little disposition to hunger so soon after a plentiful repast at home.

Could this loss of appetite explain why today's roads are not crowded with charvolants?

Pocock promoted the use of kites for various other things, including rescues. To demonstrate his ideas he put his young daughter Martha in an armchair and flew her up to the top of a high cliff. She survived the ordeal, and went on to become the mother of the cricketer W.G. Grace. However, kites could not provide power to run machinery.

Water power

Windmills are useless when the wind dies down, and also when it blows with gale force, but as long as the breeze is moderate they are good for grinding corn and raising water for irrigation – the sort of tasks that do not have to be done continuously. As long as it neither freezes nor runs dry, water is more continuous than wind, and so water wheels generated more reliable power for industry. When he built the world's first single-purpose mill in 1771, Richard Arkwright chose to do so at Cromford in Derbyshire, where he could use water power from a warm stream that came straight out of the hill, so that it never dried up in summer, and never froze in winter.

As a result, his cotton-spinning machines were known as water frames; they turned what had been a highly skilled task into child's play, and he then employed children to operate them. A spinner could spin only one thread at a time, or perhaps a dozen with the tricky Spinning Jenny, but on the water frame a child could spin 96 threads simultaneously.

Thus the water wheel was a major force in the early stages of the industrial revolution, but as people invented more complex processes and bigger factories they also wanted more power, and power even where there was no river or stream to provide it. The answer was the steam engine.

The steam engine

There is a myth that the steam engine was invented by James Watt, but the first practical machine was patented 38 years before Watt was born – in the year that his father was born: 1698. What's more, it wasn't invented in London, Manchester or Birmingham. No, the first effective machine for 'raising water by the impellant force of fire' was invented at Shilston Barton in South Devon, by Thomas Savery.

He was an enthusiastic inventor. In 1696 he took out a patent for both a machine for polishing glass and marble and another for 'rowing of ships with greater ease and expedicion then hath hitherto beene done by any other'. This seems to have been a capstan attached to paddle wheels – a sort of seventeenth-century pedalo.

In those days patents were all issued by the King. Luckily Savery knew King William III – William of Orange – and William liked his rowing machine; so Savery got a patent – but the Navy turned it down, which made him really cross.

Thomas Savery seems to have been a military engineer, and he must have known about all the local mines, especially the tin mines in Cornwall. The miners had a real problem: because the mines had been worked since Roman times the surface seams had been worked out, and, when the miners dug down, the mines filled up with water. To begin with they baled it out by hand, then they used horses, but in all deep mines this was impractical.

According to legend, Savery was pondering the problem of the flooded mines one evening after dinner, when he threw his wine bottle on the fire, saw the last of the wine inside turning into steam, and in a flash of brilliance realised the steam must be pushing the air out of the bottle. He grabbed the bottle and thrust the neck into a bowl of water. As it came into contact with the cold water in the neck, the steam in the bottle condensed, creating a vacuum, and the water climbed up inside. Savery realised that, if a wine bottle could pull water up out of a bowl, then a bigger bottle could pull water up out of the mines. In other words, he invented a steam engine.

He made a model, showed it to the King, and got himself another patent. He also demonstrated his machine to the Royal Society, on 14 June 1699. The patent has no diagram or even a description of the engine, but in 1702 he published a book called *The miner's friend – or an engine to raise water by fire, described – and of the manner of fixing it in mines, with an account of the several other uses it is applicable to; and an answer to the objections made against it.*

The book is a wonderful mixture – first a crawling letter to the King, who I reckon Savery must have thought was rather short-sighted, since the bit addressed to him starts with very big print! Then there is a chapter addressed to the Royal Society, and a 10-page sales pitch to the Gentlemen Adventurers in the Mines of England.

He followed this with a diagram and instructions – just as you might get for a video machine today. First installation, then operation, step by step: for example, page 15:

> **Light the Fire at B. When the water in N boils, the Handle of the Regulator mark'd Z must be thrust from you as far as twill go, which makes all the steam rising from the water in L pass with irresistible Force through O into P, pushing out the Air before it, through the Clack R making a noise as it goes. And when all is gone out, the Bottom of the Vessel P will be very hot.**

The way the Savery engine worked was really quite simple. There were no moving parts apart from the taps.

First he raised steam in the boiler. Then he passed steam into his working vessel, allowing it to blow out through the downpipe into the water in the bottom of the mine. He knew when the whole system was hot, and therefore full of steam, because it came clattering out of the bottom of the pipe.

Then he closed the tap between the boiler and the working vessel, so that no more steam came in, and if necessary he cooled the outside of the vessel. This caused the steam inside to condense, creating a partial vacuum, and so the pressure of the atmosphere pushed water up the lower pipe until the vessel was full. At this point he closed the tap below the vessel, opened the tap between it and the up-pipe, and also opened the tap from the boiler to admit more steam. As the steam pressure built up it pushed all the water from the vessel up the pipe to the top of the mine.

Savery was at pains to say how powerful his engine was, and he actually invented the term 'horsepower' – deliberately making it rather more than most horses could manage so that his customers would not be disappointed. However, there were three serious problems with the Savery engine. First, every time he let steam into his vessel it was condensing rapidly, first because the vessel itself was cold and second because it was full of cold water. This meant that much of the heat supplied to the boiler was wasted in warming up the water that was being pumped out of the mine.

In his book, Savery describes vividly what happened when the machine worked:

> On the outside of the vessel you may see how the water goes out, as if the vessel were transparent. For as the steam continues within the vessel, so far is the vessel dry without, and so very hot as scarce to endure the least touch of the hand. But as far as

> the water is, the said vessel will be cold and wet,
> where any water has fallen on it; which cold and
> moisture vanishes as fast as the steam, in its
> descent, takes place of the water.

The second problem was that the second stage of the process needed high-pressure steam to push the water uphill. The soldered joints were scarcely capable of holding high-pressure steam at this time; they frequently sprang leaks, and the machines rarely ran for long without needing repairs. The third problem was that they could raise water only about 40 feet (12 metres) altogether, because with a poor vacuum water will rise only about 20 feet (6 metres) – even with a perfect vacuum the theoretical maximum height is 34 feet (10 metres) – and the high-pressure side had strict limits. As a result they had to be installed far down the mine shaft, and a deep mine, say 300 feet (90 metres), would have needed a series of engines to raise the water to the top.

A few Savery engines were probably installed in mines. One was built to control the water supply at Hampton Court. Another at Campden House in Kensington was still running 18 years later. But basically it was a practical failure. Nevertheless, the Savery engine was the first practical use of steam power, and under Captain Savery's patent the steam engine came of age.

Curiously, his idea seems to have been reinvented 200 years later by four Egyptians, who in 1899 took out a patent for an apparatus for raising water. Their scheme

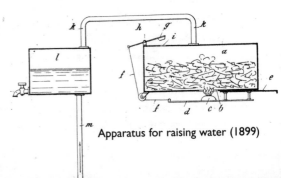

Apparatus for raising water (1899)

was to make a small fire in a box, then shut off its air supply so that it would go out, creating a partial vacuum, which would pull water up into a reservoir. This is exactly the principle of the lower half of the Savery pump!

However, back in the 1700s, the first reliable and widely used steam engine was the one invented by Thomas Newcomen of Dartmouth (see next page). Like Savery, Newcomen condensed steam to make a vacuum, but, whereas Savery had used that vacuum just to pull the water up, Newcomen made his vacuum inside a cylinder, and used it to pull down a piston. Then he used a big lever (k) to transfer the force to the pump shaft (m) which went down the mine. His first working engine about which we have reliable information was installed at a coal mine at Dudley Castle in 1712 – that is 24 years before James Watt was born. It had a cylinder 21 inches (53 centimetres) in diameter and nearly 8 feet (2.4 metres) long, and it worked at 12 strokes a minute, raising 10 gallons (45 litres) of water from a depth of 156 feet (48 metres), which corresponds to about $5\frac{1}{2}$ horse power.

By the time Thomas Newcomen died in 1729 there were 100 of his engines working all over Britain, and also in France, Belgium, Holland, Sweden, Hungary, Germany and Austria. They were manufactured for more than a hundred years. A Newcomen engine was used in Barnsley until 1934. In 1714 a Newcomen engine cost about £1,000 – a fortune. Most people couldn't afford this much, and one chap who tried said:

That cursed engine pumped my pockets dry
And left no fire to warm my fingers by!

The standard deal was to rent an engine at £7 a week, which is 35 per cent – a good rate of return. But Newcomen didn't get rich. Savery's patent, which by the Fire Engine Act of 1698 had been extended until 1733, covered all engines

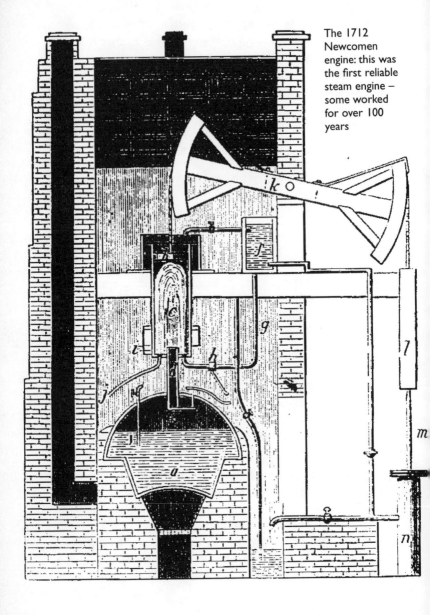

The 1712 Newcomen engine: this was the first reliable steam engine – some worked for over 100 years

that raised water by fire, and said:

> If any person or persons ... shall at any time ...
> presume to make, imitate, use, or exercise any
> vessells or engines for raiseing water or occasioning
> motion to any sort of millwork by the impellant force
> of fire, he or they shall forfeite to the said Thomas
> Savery ... all and every such vessells and engines ...

So Newcomen was forced to go into partnership with
Savery, and seems never to have made much from his
fantastic invention, although Savery did give him some
shares.

What was worse, the scientific establishment would not
believe that a provincial ironmonger could have invented
such an amazing machine; so he got no scientific credit at all.
They said he had pinched other people's ideas and made
advances by sheer luck.

However, Newcomen built the first working engines, and
when James Watt improved them towards the end of the
eighteenth century, steam engines became the workhorses of
the industrial revolution.

The Brunels' gaz engine

Knowing the tremendous power of the steam engine, many
engineers tried their skill with a variety of related systems.
Marc Isambard Brunel, the expatriate French designer of the
blockmaking machines which took over the manufacture of
pulley blocks for the Navy, and his flamboyant son Isambard
Kingdom Brunel had a grand scheme for a 'gaz engine'. Marc
had heard in an 1823 Royal Society lecture that Michael
Faraday had combined sulphuric acid and carbonate of
ammonia to produce a gas that could be liquefied but exerted

A disappointed man: Marc Isambard Brunel

enormous pressure, which rose rapidly with temperature.

Marc and Isambard wanted to use this pressure to power an engine, and they set about experiments at Rotherhithe, while wrestling with the terrible disasters of the Thames tunnel. Isambard dreamed of becoming rich and famous as a result of the gaz engine. As he wrote in his diary on 19 October 1827:

> This is a favourite 'Castle in the Air' of mine. Make the Gaz engine answer, fit out some vessels (of course a war), take some prizes, nay, some fortified town, get employed by Government contract and command a fine fleet ... Build a splendid manufactory for Gaz engines, a yard for building the boats, and at last be rich.

But it was not to be: they found there was no economic advantage over steam, and on 30 January 1833 Isambard wrote:

> All the time and expense, both *enormous,* devoted to this thing for nearly ten years are therefore *wasted* ... It must therefore die and with it all my fine hopes – crash – gone – well, well, it can't be helped.

Internal combustion

Sir George Cayley, busily designing aircraft in the early nineteenth century, also experimented with gunpowder engines, as did Denis Papin, and Edmund Cartwright, the Leicestershire vicar who invented the power loom. They all had the same idea, which was to generate a vacuum, as in the Newcomen and Watt steam engines, but to do so very quickly.

They knew that, when gunpowder explodes, all the powder turns to hot gas. If this could be made to happen inside a working cylinder the explosion would first drive the piston out, and blow out all the air from the cylinder. As the hot gas cooled a part vacuum would be formed, which could be used to do work by pulling the piston back in – or rather the pressure of the atmosphere would push it back in.

So here in principle was an engine with two working strokes. However, getting gunpowder to behave in a controllable way inside a cylinder proved immensely difficult, and no working gunpowder engine appeared. Nevertheless, the idea was born of an internal-combustion engine – an engine in which fuel could be burned not outside the boiler as with steam engines, but inside the working cylinder, where it would be most efficient.

Eventually, at the end of the nineteenth century, the potential of oil was recognised, and the oil companies discovered how to make petrol, or gasoline, with which the engineers really could get 100 horsepower into a pint pot, and the first cars were built by Otto Benz and others. However, even then some amazing mistakes were made. Herr Rudolph Diesel tried to build an internal combustion engine to run on coal dust, before he started using the fuel that is now called after him!

The Stirling engine

However, external combustion was not dead, for in 1816 an entirely new kind of engine was invented and patented by a Scottish minister, the Rev. Robert Stirling. The history of his invention is rather mysterious, for Stirling seems to have had no sort of engineering training, apart from the fact that his brother was an engineer. He took out the patent for his engine within days of becoming minister at Galston parish church, southwest of Glasgow, where he remained for the rest of his working life, and, according to a generous plaque in the church, was devoted to the welfare of his flock.

Despite this devotion, he somehow found the time to develop and improve his engine, which works on a principle analogous to the steam engine. In a typical steam engine of the Boulton & Watt type, the power is provided by a piston being pushed through a cylinder by a difference in steam pressure. The high-pressure side typically had a pressure of one atmosphere before 1800 and three atmospheres after 1800; the low-pressure side had a pressure of perhaps half an atmosphere before 1800 and one atmosphere afterwards.

The Stirling engine also has a piston driven through a cylinder, but by air rather than steam. One side of the piston is often open to the atmosphere; the other side is in contact with a fixed quantity of air that is alternately heated to raise the pressure – and make it expand – and then cooled to lower the pressure, and make it contract. The air is heated by any convenient external heat source, which means that it can be run on wood or coal, on petrol or oil or gas. Small Stirling engines will even work on the heat from a cup of tea.

Stirling engines have been used in a number of ways: they have been installed to drive church organs, because they can run very quietly; they have been run backward, to extract heat, in cryogenic work – i.e. making things cold. They have been used to drive Swedish submarines, and they have even been considered by NASA (National Aeronautics and Space Administration) engineers for driving small vehicles on Mars, using heat from the sun. However, they have never been found generally useful in such applications as road vehicles. One of the reasons for this is that they suffer from a volume/surface-area problem.

Small Stirling engines can be highly effective, which is how they can run on the heat from a cup of tea, but if you want to do any useful work you have to increase the size of the engine by, say, ten times. When its length increases by ten times, the surface area increases by a hundred times, and the volume increases by a thousand times. Because the engine contains a thousand times as much air, you need a thousand times as much heat to warm it up, but the area has increased by only a hundred times, which means that to heat the air by the same amount is much more difficult. In other words, scaling the engine up inevitably makes it less effective.

So the engine invented by the Rev. Robert Stirling in 1816 was not really a failure, but it has not proved a great success either – at least, not yet.

Electricity

Before leaving problematic power, I must just tell you about Herr Rudolph Diesel's 1897 patent to bring power to balloons. He proposed to chase after the balloon with a truck running on electrically charged rails and to supply electricity to the balloon by using an extension lead hundreds of feet long. He dismissed previous plans, to have an electric truck towing the balloon or an electric balloon towing the truck, and insisted on having both balloon and truck free to move independently, with a spring-loaded mechanism to lengthen or shorten the extension lead as required, and to prevent it from hanging in loops.

Diesel seems sometimes to have been rather optimistic in his plans, for even if the truck had not run into a river or some insurmountable obstacle in pursuit of the balloon, and even if the cable had not snagged on a tree or a building, then the loss of power in an enormously long trailing lead would almost certainly have rendered the invention virtually useless!

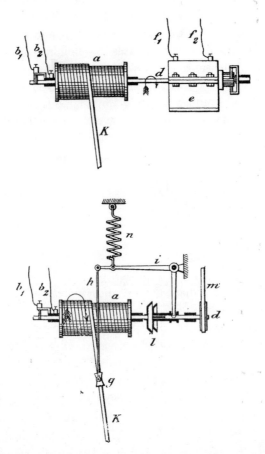

A leading design or just a basket case? Diesel's spring-loaded mechanism for 'Improvements in Supplying Electrical Energy to Electrically Propelled Aerial Machines and Balloons' (1897)

5 Perpetual motion?

As soon as people began to make machines they must have dreamed of machines that would work for nothing – clever devices that would operate on their own, grinding corn or pumping water from the well. By the Middle Ages the hunt for perpetuum mobile *had become a kind of mechanics' quest, like the hunt for the Holy Grail or the philosopher's stone that would turn everything to gold – and just like those other quests this one seemed to be impossible in practice.*

Imagine a heavy flywheel, perfectly balanced, that once set spinning goes on and on. If there were no friction and no air resistance, it would surely spin for ever – and that would be perpetual motion. A more useful flywheel would be one that could spin with such energy that it could drive millwheels and still spin for ever. This would seem to be more difficult to build, but could it perhaps be achieved by some clever arrangement of cogs, or clever use of gravity?

The desire to invent a perpetual-motion machine has certainly kept inventors going round in circles

Magic wheels

Among the earliest and best-known designs was the wheel with curved spokes fitted with sliding weights, or with ball bearings that ran along the spokes in grooves. The idea is that, as each spoke passes the top, the weight runs to the outside, and as each spoke gets to the bottom the weight returns to

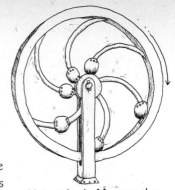

Not a wheel of fortune: the fallacy of perpetual motion (c. 1638)

the centre, so that there is always more weight on the right-hand side of the wheel, which therefore spins clockwise.

This was probably the basic design of a famous engine built by Edward Somerset, the second Marquis of Worcester, who was a friend of Charles I (his father had been made a marquis after giving the King vast amounts of money). The Marquis had an exciting life: he fought in the Civil War, was banished in 1648 and spent four years in France, was captured when he came back to England, and was imprisoned in the Tower of London for two years until Cromwell let him out.

The Marquis's wheel, which he demonstrated to the King before the Civil War, in 1638 or 1639, was 14 feet in diameter and had 40 sliding weights of 50 pounds (23 kilos) each. As he explained in his book *Century of Inventions* (published in 1663 and dedicated to Charles II), it was built:

> To provide and make that all the Weights of the descending side of a Wheel shall be perpetually further from the Centre than those of the mounting side, and yet equal in number ... A most incredible thing, if not seen, but tried before the late King (of blessed memory) in the Tower, by my directions, two Extraordinary Embessadors accompanying His

He allegedly experimented with a version of this wheel known as the 'water-commanding engine', also described as a 'hydraulic machine', on the walls of his home, Raglan Castle, and it was said to be able to 'raise to the height of forty feet, by the strength of one man and in the space of one minute of time, four large buckets of water'. There is also a suggestion that the same machine had the power of 'driving up water by fire', and as a result some people have claimed that the Marquis invented the steam engine! In 1663 Worcester managed to get through an Act of Parliament which gave him a monopoly of the profits from his machine. He promised to pay 10 per cent to the King, and hoped to pay off his debts with the rest. However, cynical Robert Hooke – who was curator of experiments at the Royal Society, and who formulated the famous Hooke's law (of elasticity) – described his engine as 'one of the perpetual-motion fallacies'.

The Marquis was an enthusiastic inventor, however, and was not likely to have been put off by a rude comment from Robert Hooke. His 1661 patent, couched in the most curious language, describes a variety of improbable-sounding clocks, guns, carriages and boats. The first of these modest proposals was for a watch or clock that would keep perfect time without having to be wound up – another impressive claim of perpetual motion. Unfortunately, those early patents were not provided with any explanation or diagrams, so we have no idea how he proposed to bring about the miracles he promised.

A clever variant of the Marquis's wheel was the wheel with hinged spokes, like elbows. As each spoke passed the top the weighted 'hand' would swing over, increasing the turning moment or torque, so that again the wheel should revolve clockwise. This idea is at least 600 years old, for

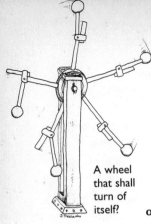

Henry Dircks, writing about perpetual motion in 1861, gives an account of an invention by the early thirteenth century architect Wilars (or Villand) de Honnecourt, who said:

A wheel that shall turn of itself?

Many a time have skilful workmen tried to contrive a wheel that shall turn of itself; here is a way to do it by means of an uneven number of mallets ...

Wind and water

Five hundred years ago, the Italian philosopher and alchemist Mark Anthony Zimara designed an elegant perpetual-motion system – a windmill whose output drove giant bellows in order to make wind to drive the windmill.

Then there were designs based on the flow of water or some other liquid – perhaps quicksilver, as mercury was called. The simplest plan was a cleverly shaped funnel; the greater weight of liquid in the wide part of the funnel was supposed to push the liquid through so that it ran right over the top and back into the funnel again – and on the way it could drive a water wheel, which would do useful work. Unfortunately what actually happens is that water reaches the same level in both sides of the vessel, regardless of the width of the tubes. The pressure depends only on the depth, not on the weight of water.

The perpetual-motion wind machine was not something to bellow about

A more complex design would use
the flow of water from a cistern to turn
a water-wheel, use some of the energy
from the water wheel to pump the
water back up, and use the rest to do
useful work; the English physician
Robert Fludd described such an
arrangement in 1618, using an
Archimedes' screw to pump the water
up, and grinding corn with the surplus
energy. Alas, in real life the water wheel
cannot supply enough energy to pump
the water back up to the top.

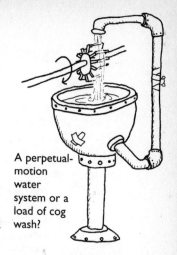

A perpetual-
motion
water
system or a
load of cog
wash?

An entirely different type of machine was described at
length, and with full scientific detail, by the Swiss
mathematician Johann Bernoulli. This depended on the fact
that two different liquids may mix completely with one
another and yet have quite different densities. He did not
specify the liquids, but water and alcohol mix, and have
different densities; so in principle the machine should run on
brandy. The brandy is placed in a tall tank which contains a
narrow vertical tube. At the bottom of the tube is a special
filter that allows alcohol but not water to pass through – rather
like the semipermeable membranes of cell walls, which allow
water to pass through but not sugars.

When the tank was full, Bernoulli said, alcohol would flow
through the filter and fill the narrow tube, and, because alcohol
is less dense than water, the alcohol would fill the tube to a
greater depth than the water. In fact the density of alcohol is
only 0.8 grams per millilitre; so if the depth of the water were
20 centimetres the depth of the alcohol would be 25
centimetres – in other words the alcohol would rise 5
centimetres above the water. Therefore the narrow tube could
be arranged so that the alcohol flowed out and back into the

large container, driving a wheel on the way.

Sad to say, Bernoulli failed to explain just what filter will pass alcohol but not water …

Sir William Congreve – the man who designed rockets for the army in the early 1800s, burned Boulogne to the ground by mistake in 1806, and founded the Royal Artillery Rocket Brigade – invented in 1827 a perpetual-motion machine of some subtlety. An endless band of sponge is looped round a triangle of rollers, and is in turn surrounded by an endless heavy chain. The bottom side of the triangle dips into a reservoir of water, which soaks into the sponge by capillary action.

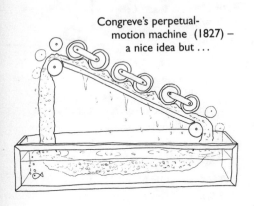

Congreve's perpetual-motion machine (1827) – a nice idea but ...

Without the heavy chain the water in the vertical and sloping sides would balance, but the heavy chain squashes all the water out of the sponge. This makes the vertical sponge (unsquashed) heavier, and so the sponge and the chain move round anticlockwise. Or at least they should. But alas they don't.

Magnetic motion

Alexander Bain, inventor of the fax machine (see page 107), spent a good deal of time and money trying to make a perpetual-motion machine, probably using the newfangled techniques of electricity and magnetism, which must have seemed almost like magic. However, the idea was not new.

In his classic book *De magnete*, published in 1600, William

Gilberd talked about making perpetual motion by using magnets, and he was a bright chap; the great Italian scientist Galileo said of Gilberd:

> **I extremely praise, admire, and envy this author, for that a conception so stupendous should come into his mind...**

and the poet John Dryden said:

> **Gilberd shall live till lodestones cease to draw.**

In 1648 the Bishop of Chester described a system in which a lodestone magnet would pull a steel ball up a slope:

> **which steel as it ascends near to the lodestone may be contrived to fall through some hole in the plane, and so return to the place from whence at first it began to move; and being there the lodestone will again attract it upward till coming to the hole it will fall down again; and so the motion will be perpetual ...**

The great Sir David Brewster, inventor of the kaleidoscope, was fooled in 1818 by a magnetically driven machine that apparently achieved perpetual motion. The sad thing is that none of these machines has worked, nor will any such machine.

The person who first began to think clearly about the nature of energy and especially heat was James Prescott Joule, who worked in Salford in the 1840s and 1850s. He measured how much heat was generated when he used various machines to do work, and he concluded that energy can neither be created nor destroyed.

Joule said:

> The grand agents of Nature are by the Creator's fiat indestructible; whenever mechanical force is expended an exact equivalent of heat is always obtained ... It is manifestly absurd to suppose that the powers with which God has endowed matter can be destroyed any more than they can be created by man's agency.

In other words, though for somewhat unscientific reasons, James Prescott Joule was the first person to recognise the conservation of energy.

Joule's work led to the whole science of thermodynamics, whose laws were gradually sorted out in Scotland, France, Germany and England, during the second half of the nineteenth century. The laws of thermodynamics turn out to be universal and unbreakable; they are some of the most fundamental laws of nature, and there is no way round them. The First Law says that energy cannot be created or destroyed, which means that even if perpetual motion were possible – suppose a wheel could spin without any friction or air resistance, for example – no useful energy could be taken out of the system. In other words, the wheel could not do any work without slowing down.

This turns out to have a simple common-sense analogy. Suppose I were to go on my bike from the top of Ben Nevis to sea level at Fort William, five miles away. I would have descended 4,400 feet (1,340 metres) – which corresponds to the potential energy I have lost.

Now suppose I go the wrong way up the Great Glen, and from the top of Ben Nevis ride via Inverness, Aberdeen, Arbroath, Dundee and Perth to the sea at Fort William, I shall still have descended 4,400 feet, however many mountains and valleys I have crossed in between. So the change in height – or energy – is the same, regardless of the path I take.

And, if I go back to the top of Ben Nevis, I shall have climbed 4,400 feet, whichever way I go. Then, having completed a circuit, I shall have descended a total of zero feet, used zero potential energy in total. Whenever any system completes a cycle and gets back to where it started, the total energy change must be zero. And that means that no perpetual-motion machine, however it is built, can deliver energy and carry on going at the same speed, because when it gets back to where it started it must either have all its original energy, or have given some of it up and have less of its own. A simple way of stating the First Law is 'You can't win!'

In real life, there is always friction when any parts are moving. To overcome this friction takes energy, which is converted to heat. As a result, the machine must slow down, since its energy is being used up.

The Second Law of thermodynamics is even more brutal; 'You can't even break even!' Long before thermodynamics had been dreamed up, good scientists recognised that perpetual motion is impossible. Newton implied it in his great book *Principia*, published in 1687, and the Parisian Academy of Sciences refused in 1775 to accept any more perpetual-motion schemes. However, the lure of finding a magical source of energy remained irresistible. Even though the laws of thermodynamics were well understood by about 1900, they have not prevented people from going on trying to find ways round them.

The first British patent for a perpetual-motion machine was granted in 1635, and by 1903 there were 600 patents; now the British Patent Office will not accept perpetual-motion applications. Every year the US Patent Office receives about a hundred patent applications for perpetual-motion machines, even though they insist on working models; they now send this response to those who submit such applications:

> The views of the Patent Office are in accord with those scientists who have investigated the subject and are to the effect that such devices are physical impossibilities. The position of the Office can only be rebutted by a working model. ... The Office hesitates to accept fees from applicants who believe they have discovered Perpetual Motion, and deems it only fair to give such applicants a word of warning that fees cannot be recovered after the case has been considered by the Examiner.

Even so, people are not discouraged. In his page on the World Wide Web, A.E. Wilcox writes:

> Most people discount perpetual motion devices, because they believe that ALL such devices break either the first or second law of thermodynamics. My device doesn't break either. It's what some might/should call a perpetual motion device of the third kind. Let me stress that just because all known perpetual motion devices have broken the first or second law, doesn't imply that all possible perpetual motion devices must break the first or second law.

Perpetual-motion machines are as impossible as the magic stone that turneth all to gold, but, if you want to try to make one, good luck!

6 Batty bicycles

The history of the bicycle is shrouded in mist, confusion and argument, which seems curious, since it is such a simple and useful form of transport. We actually know much more about early trains and aircraft than we do about early bicycles. His notebooks suggest that Leonardo da Vinci dreamed of a bicycle, and his dream is so close to the modern form that it is hard to believe that hundreds of years went by before the machine was actually built.

Horse-drawn carriages were used by the Romans, and by early Britons – Boudicca had one with knives on the wheels. Ox carts were routinely used for transport during the Middle Ages. There were tricycles in the eighteenth century: the Scottish engineer William Murdoch built himself a tricycle to go to school in Ayrshire in the 1760s, for

Bicycle from the notebooks of Leonardo da Vinci – although some experts believe this particular sketch was added centuries after Leonardo's death

85

example. Steam carriages came into use in the early 1800s, and by the 1830s railways were snaking across the country. How is it possible that no one had by then invented the bicycle, which is a far simpler machine?

Perhaps it would have been too expensive for the working man, and even more so for women, while the upper classes would have been appalled at the idea of having to propel themselves by their own efforts. Nevertheless, I am amazed that the first bicycle did not appear until 1839, and the bicycle as we know it not until the 1860s and later.

The invention of the bicycle

In 1817 Karl von Drais patented what came to be known as the hobby horse – a bench balanced on two wheels. You sat astride it and pushed along on the ground with your feet. This tended to wear out the shoe leather, and even the iron-soled shoes that were made, but nevertheless enjoyed a brief popularity in the 1820s, when everyone who was anyone had to have one.

The next giant leap forward had to be a leap in the imagination, to grasp the idea that it might be possible to balance on two wheels without keeping both feet on the ground! As far as we know, this idea was first put into practice in 1839 – in the shape of a wooden-framed machine with wooden wheels – by a Scottish blacksmith, Kirkpatrick MacMillan, at Courthill Smithy in the parish of Keir about 14 miles north of Dumfries. Kirkpatrick MacMillan was born in Keir in September 1812, and became a blacksmith like his dad. He probably went off to work in a foundry in Glasgow, returned to Keir, and took over the business when his dad retired in 1851.

In the 1860s pedal-driven bicycles were made by

Big wheels were good for rough ground and for speed

Michaux in Paris; they were called boneshakers or velocipedes, depending on whether you were more impressed by their painfulness or their speed. The 'ordinary' – the high bicycle, or penny-farthing – came along about 1870. This was a sensible development. Drive to those early bikes was by pedals attached directly to the front wheel. There were no gears, and usually no brakes; you slowed down by back-pedalling.

Most of the people who took to the bicycle wanted to go fast, to get from A to B in a hurry, and to impress their friends, and the speed of a bicycle with direct drive

A bicycle made for two (1869)

depended directly on the size of the driving wheel. With a front wheel six feet across you could go three times as fast as with one two feet across.

There were considerable disadvantages to this. Getting on to a high bicycle is tricky. I know: I have done it. You need either a mounting block as used for getting on to a horse or a good deal of courage and skill to push forward, put one foot on the footrest low down, and then vault into the saddle as the bike moves off. Riding also is nerve-racking, since you are perched about six feet, or a couple of metres, off the ground, which feels extremely high.

Once going, the high bicycle is much more stable than a modern bike, because the huge front wheel gives you so much rotational inertia – it's like a great flywheel which once spinning is extremely hard to twist. So I am told you can ride with your hands off the handlebars at 2 m.p.h. However, if you hit a serious bump or pothole you go straight over the front wheel and land on your face from a great height. Many cyclists were injured this way.

And even getting off is an acquired skill. After slowing down by back-pedalling you ease out of the saddle, step back down on to the tiny footrest, allowing the bicycle to move away from under you, and then gently step down on to the ground – at least that is the theory.

Partly because it was so terrifying, and partly because it was so fast, the high bicycle was tremendously popular with the young men who were the most enthusiastic cyclists in the 1870s and 80s. Its demise started quite suddenly on 18 May 1889, when Willie Hume appeared for a race on the Queen's College playing fields in Belfast. Everyone laughed at him, for, while all the other riders had high bicycles, he was on a safety bicycle, with the silly pneumatic tyres recently constructed by the local vet, a certain John Boyd Dunlop. The spectators stopped laughing when Hume won the race, and suddenly everyone wanted the new tyres, and the high bicycle began to go out of fashion.

So that was how modern bicycles developed, but what about the MacMillan machine? It had a massive, heavy, wooden frame, reminiscent of the hobby horse, and wooden wheels like cartwheels, bound with iron tyres. The front wheel was steered with handlebars, more or less as on a modern bike. But the propulsion system looks distinctly odd to modern eyes. There were cranks on the back wheel, and from them treadles came forward to hang beside the front wheel. You put your feet on the treadles, and propelled the bike by pushing forward with alternate feet (instead of pushing down, as on modern pedals). Pedalling it, sliding the feet to and fro, reminded me of when my dancing partner tried to teach me the tango… And steering is tricky because the treadles prevent the front wheel from turning more than about 20 degrees.

Apparently the original machine weighed half a hundredweight (25 kilos), and MacMillan frequently rode the 14 miles into Dumfries in less than an hour – which is impressive, to say the least. Critics say MacMillan's machine was not the precursor of the modern bike. Drive to the back wheels didn't come into serious use for another 40 years, and the treadles were a blind alley.

What's more, there isn't much evidence that MacMillan really built and rode such a machine – except an article in the *Glasgow Argus* of 1842 which said that a gentleman of Dumfriesshire had ridden 40 miles from Old Cumnock to Glasgow – in five hours – and there, in a crowd of spectators, had mounted the pavement and knocked over a small child. Luckily the child was unhurt and the gentleman was fined only five shillings (25 pence). Unfortunately the article does not mention MacMillan by name – and he was not a gentleman – nor does it say that the velocipede was a bicycle.

Superior saddles

Whether or not MacMillan's machine was a failed invention, and whether or not it was the true precursor of the modern bicycle, when the bicycle really arrived, in the 1880s, it spawned a mass of new inventions, some for radical new types of bicycle and some for outlandish accessories.

Probably the most common of these were for new saddle designs, which came in all shapes and sizes. Take for example the clever idea of Frederick William Barratt, ironmonger of Wimborne, who was probably worried about his wife's safety, and in 1899 patented a saddle 'of the ordinary or hygienic pattern but in the front centre of peak I introduce a wheel or roller of suitable material, grooved or otherwise. The object is to facilitate mounting and dismounting and to entirely obviate the danger caused by the dress catching. The wheel or roller ... revolves as the rider gets on and off the saddle.'

He went on to explain:

> It is well known that ladies attain or mount the saddle by an upward and backward spring movement, at the same time pressing forward with the foot upon one pedal. This action causes a considerable pressure upon the peak of saddle as the dress glides over same and it is not infrequent that in doing so with the ordinary saddle the dress catches with more or less risk of falling.
>
> A further difficulty experienced by a large number of female cyclists is the fact that they are compelled to fix the saddle too low, owing to their inability to spring into the saddle when it is at its proper height in consequence of the friction of the ordinary peak, and suffer thereby from what is known as knee cramp. My invention entirely obviates the danger of the dress catching and greatly facilitates the mounting, doing away with these two objectionable features of the ordinary saddle.

Sadly, Mr Barratt's idea did not seem to catch on, and women's saddles still tend to be something of a problem, although nowadays women usually ride wearing trousers or cycling shorts, rather than voluminous dresses.

Some of these 'improved' saddle designs were rather trivial, and reflected concern for the body's tender spots, or as one patentee put it 'the organic parts'; others were ludicrously complex, but for me they provide a sort of window into the Victorian mind. Here is a problem – a slightly irritating thing like an uncomfortable cycle saddle – so let's invent something to fix it. The Victorian age was the age of machines of all sorts, from steam carriages to aircraft, and the idea of a machine to solve each problem was firmly rooted in tne fertile Victorian mind. It was also the age of the entrepreneur, and many of the inventors rushed to the Patent Office to protect their brainchildren. Just leafing through the old patents provides some fascinating insights.

George Augustus Youngman, manager of St Stephen's Cycle Works in Norwich, patented a new form of saddle by connecting the peak or fore-end with the underframe, 'as to more effectually distribute the stress on the leather or other flexible material from which the said seating is formed, and thereby to provide for the greater comfort of the rider'.

Joseph Fowler Steele and Harry Vaughan Currie, of the Albion Mills Saddlery Company in Birmingham, interposed under the leather upper 'a pad of stiffer leather and also a pad of felt or india-rubber, or like material, for the purpose of distributing the weight and of affording a more comfortable seat for the rider'. They also included 'a central supporting spring or supplementary elastic support of such resistance as to prevent undue or inconvenient deflection of the central part of the saddle seat, but to yield sufficiently under the motion of the cycle to absorb any jarring or like action'.

One of the most amazing inventions I have come across for the improvement of cycle saddles was a device dreamed up by a retired tea planter, Richard Wade Jenkins. He claimed this would also be able to maintain a constant level on ships at sea (reminiscent of Bessemer's boat – page 20). The basic idea

A tricycle
made for
two
(1883)

was simple: a shallow watertight tank filled with water or
other incompressible fluid was bolted to the saddle or other
platform to be kept level, and supported on pistons which
were free to slide up and down in cylinders; the pistons were
fixed by hinges to the cycle frame or boat deck. However
much the bicycle leaned or the ship rocked, he suggested, the
water would retain its own level, and the saddle or platform,
resting on the pistons, would therefore stay perfectly
horizontal. He explained the mode of action thus:

> **It is obvious that as the under part or support rests
> on the swaying ship or the like, it partakes of all the
> motions and communicates them ... to the plungers
> acting directly on the confined fluid. As the plunger**

rises, forced up by the rising deck, the pressure which it exerts upon the fluid supported above it, acts instantly through the incompressible water on the opposite falling piston, the mobile fluid thus forced from the one cylinder at once occupying exactly the same space in the opposite cylinder above the falling piston.

But insamuch as the falling piston, necessarily following the declining deck, would leave a vacuum, it is instantly followed by the fluid above it so that the opposite corresponding rising plunger, not only finds small resistance to overcome in lifting and following its superincumbent fluid, but is simultaneously urged to its work by the pressure of the atmosphere below it, thus providing the overpart with legs or supports lengthening and shortening in response to the rising and falling deck, leaving the horizontal position of the overpart unaffected.

He went on to outline how useful this horizontal platform would be for mounting light guns, searchlights, observation platforms for officers, deck-chairs, seats, benches, berths, tables and the like.

There seem to me to be a number of flaws in Mr Jenkins's argument. To begin with, why did he want to keep his cycle saddle horizontal? The sensation would be rather disconcerting, and would make it difficult to keep contact with both pedals. However, this is a small drawback compared with the fact that it clearly would not work, since there is nothing in this design to keep the saddle or platform horizontal. Indeed I reckon the moment it tipped even slightly from the horizontal, it would overbalance completely, throwing the rider wildly off balance, and casting deckchairs, guns and observing officers into the sea!

Artful accessories

Richard Singer of Leipzig in the Kingdom of Saxony, perhaps still worrying about ladies' dresses, patented a brush for cleaning bicycle chains. The two halves of the brush are clamped on to the chain, which is then pulled through to remove all the mud, oil and grease that might otherwise stain the clothes.

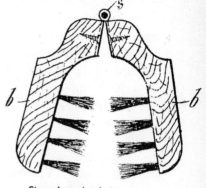

Singer's cycle-chain cleaning brush (1897)

Frank Mossberg of Attleborough, Massachusetts, produced a brilliant design for a bicycle bell in 1899. The bell was mounted on the front of the frame, just above the front wheel, and activated by a lever on the handlebars. This lever pulled a cord which pulled a coaster wheel on to the side of the front tyre – just as some dynamos are driven today. This wheel activated a pair of hammers which pounded alternately on the inside of the bell, so that it continued to ring as long as you pulled the cord and the front wheel was still turning.

Furthermore he introduced a cunning friction drive inside the bell in order to 'reduce the relative number of strokes on the bell as the speed of the bicycle is increased, as one great difficulty … is to make the ringing of the bell clear and not to have the strokes run into each other, and make a confused sound … With my improved friction motion … the number of strokes will be greatly equalised in fast or slow riding.' With or without the confused sound, I would love to have one of Mr Mossberg's bells on my bike!

The environmental demands were rather different in Sydney, in the Colony of New South Wales, where John

Howard used exactly the same sort of drive system for a bike-powered sheep-shearing machine 'specially adapted for use by small sheep farmers who do not require large installations of machine sheep shears or other similar implements'. This was simple and clever:

> **The bicycle may be ridden from shed to shed by one of the shearers, and when thus travelling, the stand E will be caused to assume the position shown by the dotted lines ... When it is desired to start work, the stand E is brought down to the position shown in the drawings, and secured by bolts or screws, to the floor of the shed, to a plank or other suitable base which may be handy. It will thus be seen that the driving wheel A of the bicycle will be raised from the ground and free to rotate without propelling the machine forward, while the friction pinion J being in close contact with the tyre, the power developed by the rider will be communicated to the axle H and thence to the sharpening disc K and the flexible shaft L at the outer end of which is the implement to which power is to be conveyed.**

He was clearly an experienced engineer, and must have tried and tested his apparatus, for he points out that 'The sharpening disc K will have a double function. It will act as a fly wheel and governor to regulate and equalise the driving speed. With a view to the same end, the tyre B, instead of being inflated with air, may be filled with water, thereby adding to the weight and increasing its momentum without increasing the speed at which it is driven.' I am not sure about riding the bike with the back tyre full of water, but otherwise this looks like an excellent piece of machinery; I almost wish I had a sheep to try it out on!

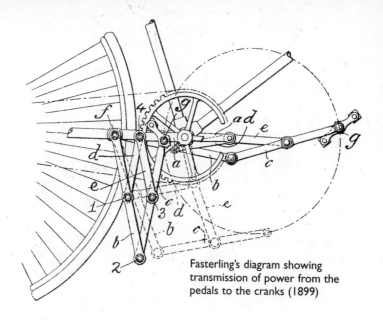

Fasterling's diagram showing transmission of power from the pedals to the cranks (1899)

Driving gear

Many patents were taken out for improved driving gear. William Francis Hackman of Uxbridge devised a system to transfer power from cranks to the driving wheel through the medium of coupling rods, housed within the backstays. Friedrich Fasterling of Prussia transmitted power from the pedals to the cranks by means of a link parallelogram; he claimed that 'by this means the pedal crank axle is driven very easily in all positions of the cranks'.

A watchmaker, Giovanni Antonio Philipon of Lima, Peru, came up with a novel design in which the cyclist pushed the pedals forward instead of downward 'by which I secure a more advantageous application of the muscular power, at the same time enabling the rider to keep his balance more easily.' Pushing forward with your feet is curiously similar to what you must do to ride the Kirkpatrick MacMillan

A unicycle (1884)

machine (page 86), and also a modern recumbent cycle, in which you lie back with your feet out in front.

Having tried both of these, I don't believe the application of muscular power is advantageous, and on Philipon's machine you would be in grave danger of fouling the front wheel with your outside foot whenever you turned a corner. It has the additional disadvantage that the immediate drive from the pedal levers to the chainwheel is by slots pushing studs as they slide past them. This is crude, inefficient and bound to cause rapid wear.

Alfred Robert Jardine from Lanarkshire chose a different method to get 'greater leverage in the application of driving force and greater ease in the propulsion of the cycle'. His complex set of levers connecting the pedals to the chainwheel seem to me to be bound to provide more friction and no gain. Using an ordinary bike with gears, you can get more 'leverage' by changing to a lower gear, while if you want longer travel for your feet you can fit longer cranks, as long as they don't hit the ground. Therefore, providing extra levers cannot help. Furthermore, the bicycle as we know it is extraordinarily efficient; when properly lubricated and set up, 98 per cent of the effort is said to go into forward propulsion. I find it hard to believe that any additional ironmongery can improve this efficiency to any significant extent.

Anyone who rides a bicycle will know that going up and down hills is rather frustrating, because, although you can get up tremendous speed going down, you can rarely use all that speed to coast up the other side; so often you have to slow down at the bottom, and then you lose most of your momentum. But perhaps this would not be so if you could only store the kinetic energy instead of wasting it all as heat, which is what happens when you apply the brakes.

A gentleman from Upper Norwood, James Stack Lauder,

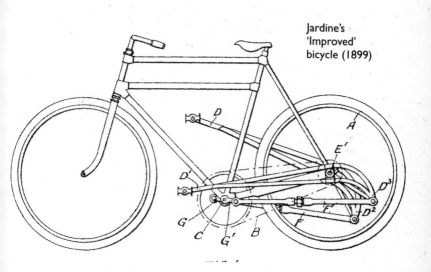

Jardine's
'Improved'
bicycle (1899)

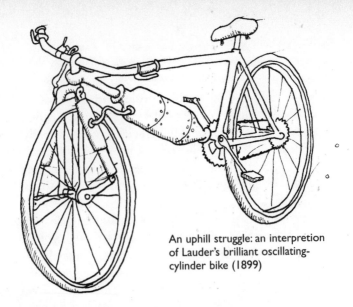

An uphill struggle: an interpretion
of Lauder's brilliant oscillating-
cylinder bike (1899)

noticed both this fact and that the bicycle is made from
hollow metal tubes, and came up with a brilliant idea.
Impractical, I think, but nevertheless brilliant.

Lauder suggested mounting a pair of oscillating cylinders,
one each side of the front wheel. As you zoom downhill,
switch these cylinders into action, so that they pull in air,
compress it, and pump it into the hollow frame. On a level
road you throw the cylinders out of gear, and use the bike
as normal, but when you are faced with an uphill stretch
you switch the cylinders into drive mode, and use the
compressed air stored in the frame to help drive the front
wheel and pull you up the hill.

An additional advantage of this system is that, when
used to compress air, the cylinders act to slow the bicycle,
'checking the rapid descent of the machine, thus avoiding
the necessity of the ordinary brake ... It is also proposed to
utilise the store of air ... to inflate the tyres, and to operate a
whistle or siren, thereby entirely dispensing with the

ordinary pump and bell.'

John Browne of Stoke Newington came up with what might perhaps be classed as a wheelchair, although he seems to have been a little optimistic about the power and stamina of the fingers. He called his contraption a 'manumotive vehicle' and said that it would provide 'a motive mechanism easily manipulated and by which gas, electric, or oil engines may be dispensed with – the mechanism itself consisting solely of gearing arranged and constructed so as to be worked by hand with the greatest facility'.

Reading these patents a hundred years after they were written, I am fairly sure that some of the machines they describe – the bike-powered sheep shearer, for example – had been built, tried and improved before the patent was applied for. Others, such as this manumotive vehicle, were simply figments of the imagination. Mr Browne has sketched – although without any constructional details – an elegantly shaped car body, with front and back seats, and therefore designed to carry at least two people. Indeed it must carry two people, since the inadequate-looking tiller for steering can be operated only from the front seat, while the person in the back seat, who would seem to have an uncomfortable half-lying position, has to supply all the driving power by twiddling a small wheel in front of the chest, using only the thumb and first finger. I estimate that to drive such a vehicle up the slightest hill would need the full force of both hands, even without anyone in the front seat, which would be a bit dangerous, since from the driving seat you could not steer …

Perhaps the most hopeful of the ingenious ideas I have come across for powering bicycles was dreamed up by a house decorator, William Bettis of West Ham; it's a 'wind motor, to assist the rider while travelling'. The notion is simple: he mounted a fan or small windmill on the front of the bike, so that, when he was pedalling along, the rush of air would turn the blades. These were arranged with gears to help turn the wheels, so that, in his words, 'when the rider mounts to go forward it sets the whole of the parts in motion, and the motor wheel is assisting the rider by its velocity and the rider is being partly propelled by the current of air that he is passing through. Thus he is receiving great ease.'

I wish I could believe it! There is a hint of perpetual motion about this scheme. In practice I reckon that a big fan on the front would enormously increase your air resistance, and make it almost impossible to do more than about 12 m.p.h. But if it actually worked then presumably you would sail off into a headwind without pedalling, and if ever you encountered a tailwind you would be in danger of going backward!

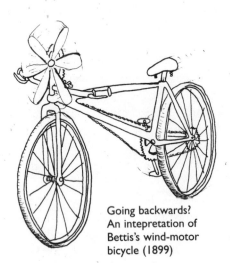

Going backwards? An intepretation of Bettis's wind-motor bicycle (1899)

Crazy constructions

Of all the bicycle patents I have seen, the prize for battiness must surely go to Paul Herrmann of Berlin, who designed a bicycle made entirely from pleated cane. The frame was to be made of cane – or at worst of cane with a wooden core. The forks were to be built from cane, and because they have 'to resist a great tendency to bending ... are constructed ... in the form of a trellis framework ... This construction provided with diagonal supports is best capable of supporting the strain to be put upon it.'

The handlebars 'are kept completely hollow, are consequently very elastic and do not convey shocks to the hands of the rider ... The saddle is formed of woven cane in the form of basket work ... [which] assures the elasticity of the same and renders the application of springs unnecessary. The wheel tyres are either twisted spirally of Spanish cane and provided with a woven covering in tubular form of split cane, or they are formed ... of several canes with the said covering twisted round a strong hemp cord ...' And he goes on to say that bicycles made like this would be cheaper, lighter, and more shock-absorbent than ordinary bicycles, and almost unbreakable!

And then there were the unicycles and the tricycles, which look wonderful in the pictures, although they have scarcely survived the test of time.

A really wooden idea: Herrmann's pleated cane cycle (1897)

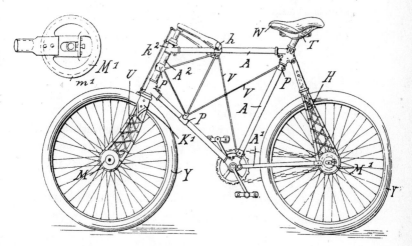

7 Before their time

This chapter is a celebration of ideas that really were good, but came too early. They have all proved their worth in the end, but when they were invented, these devices were ahead of the available technology, or of the demand, or both.

A dramatic recent example was provided in 1947 by Dennis Gabor, who was waiting for the previous players to come off the tennis court he had booked to play with Winifred Smith at St Andrew's Tennis Club in Rugby, when he suddenly said to her, 'Excuse me, I must go and write something down.' He walked purposefully away, leaving her without a game, because he had just seen how to make a hologram. He won the Nobel Prize for this brilliant invention, but it was ahead of its time, because it proved impossible actually to make a hologram until the laser was invented, some ten years later.

The gas turbine

Most of our electrical power today is generated in power stations by steam turbines, which use a variety of fuels to heat water in order to generate steam at high pressure, and then use the steam to spin vast turbines in order to generate electricity. Its close relative, the gas turbine, provides the driving power for thousands of aircraft, and seems to be a thoroughly modern invention; the jet engine as we know it was patented by Frank Whittle in 1930 and was powering an aircraft in 1941. And yet a gas turbine was patented by one John Barber more than two hundred years ago, in 1791!

Could John Barber have known what he was doing? Did his gas turbine ever work? We can only guess at the answers to these questions, but it seems from the evidence of his patent that he at least had a sensible idea. However, the technology of the time would probably have prevented his machine from working properly.

John Barber was born in 1734 at Greasley in Nottinghamshire, learned about coal mining from his uncle, John Fletcher, and eventually became colliery owner and manager somewhere in Haunchwood near Nuneaton in Warwickshire. Like most mine owners, he had problems with flooding, and two of his five patents are about draining mines. He must have known about the Newcomen engines, which had been pumping water out of mines in the Midlands since 1712, but he thought he could do better. By 1791 he was living south of Nuneaton in Attleborough, which is the address on his brilliant fourth patent of that year, which is, in his words, for 'a method of rising inflammable air for the purpose of procuring motion …'

Barber had identified two problems with the steam engine. First, it was inefficient: you have to burn fuel to heat water to make steam to make pistons go up and down – a lot of stages. Second, to do most useful jobs you have to convert the reciprocating up-and-down movement into a circular one. His grand idea was somehow to make the fuel combustion produce circular motion directly, and his patent is amazing. It describes not just a rough idea but a complete self-sustaining engine where a jet of burning gas turns a turbine which can be applied to 'Grinding, rolling, forging, spinning and every other mechanical operation'.

The problem about patents is that often they are just great ideas – not only were the inventions never built, they could never have worked. So the question is: did Barber really build the gas turbine 140 years before it was reinvented by Frank Whittle? Barber's machine has three parts: a retort to supply the gas, pumps to get it up to pressure and to pump in air, and finally the turbine itself.

His gas supply was just a retort in which he heated 'coal, wood, oil, or any other combustible matter' – but that is reasonable, since coal gas had been made that way for at least a hundred years.

What about his pump? He needed gas and air under pressure to burn properly, but gas pumps are difficult to make. He simply took a vertical pipe which contained the gas or air and had a valve at the top, and pushed it down into a larger pipe filled with water. The amazing thing is that this works: as you push the gas-filled pipe down into the other, the gas tries to push the water out, but as the water climbs up the outer tube it pushes back, creating pressure, just as Barber planned. Perhaps the cleverest idea is using the water both to create the pressure and also to make the gas-tight seals, which are the most difficult aspect of a gas pump.

Barber pumped the gas and air into a chamber called the 'exploder', where, he said, 'the two airs ... so mixed will take fire on application of a match or candle to the mouth of the exploder and rush out with great rapidity in one continued stream of fire'. And there is no doubt that coal gas and air under pressure will burn in a jet.

He said that not only could this new engine be connected up to all sorts of mechanical processes, but the 'fluid stream may be injected into furnaces for smelting metallic ores, or passed out at the stern of any ship, boat, barge, or other vessel, so as by an opposing and impelling power directed against the water carrying such vessel, the vessel with its contents may be driven in any direction whatsoever' – in other words he envisaged jet propulsion.

The practical problems were rooted in eighteenth-century technology. To get a powerful jet you need vast quantities of combustible gas – more than could easily be generated by heating coal in a kettle. And you also need to burn it under considerable pressure, whereas Barber's pumps would scarcely deliver more than two atmospheres in total. So Barber's brilliant idea was unfortunately 150 years ahead of its time.

The fax machine

During the 1960s the telephone was the instrument of the future – the most common way to get news rapidly over great distances – while the telex was used for more formal messages, and more detailed information. Then in the 1970s the fax machine arrived, and suddenly it became possible to send a whole page of text or pictures or both across the world within a minute or so; this speeded up the rate of transmission of information by at least 10 times. Now the fax itself is being superseded by e-mail and the Internet, but for some 20 years the fax machine was one of the most important pieces of equipment in most offices. Yet the fax machine was invented not in the 1970s or even the 1960s, but in the 1840s – thirty years before the telephone!

The countryside near John O'Groats is mainly bleak and desolate moorland, and the Bain family lived in a remote stone croft near Leanmore, a few miles north of Wick. Alexander Bain and his twin sister Margaret were born in October 1810. Like the other 11 children, Sandy walked to school in Backlass in the winter and worked as a shepherd in the summer.

He was bottom of the class in school and a poor shepherd too, because he was always dreaming. But he was fascinated by clocks, and made himself a model clock using

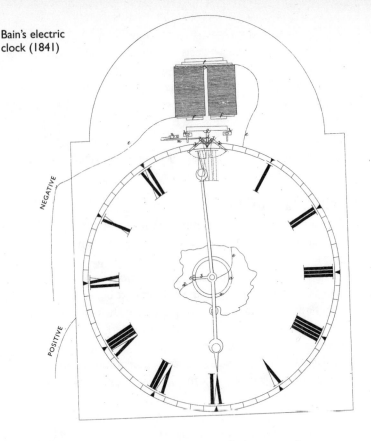

heather for the spring and the cogs. His father must have
been a man of compassion, for he arranged for Sandy to be
apprenticed to a clockmaker in Wick.

In the snow of January 1830 Alexander Bain walked 21
miles from Wick to Thurso to hear a lecture on 'Light, heat,
and the electric fluid'. The lecture changed his life, for he
decided then and there that electricity was the stuff to work
with, and he began to experiment with electrical machines.

Bain invented and patented a wide variety of curious
things – not only several types of automatic telegraph, an

electric clock, the earth battery, insulation for electric cables, and an electric fire alarm, but also a new type of hydraulic inkstand and inkholder in 1841, and in 1844 an apparatus for ascertaining and registering the progress of ships, and the temperature of their holds, for taking soundings and so on.

One of his 1841 patents covered not only a method for sending signals down a telegraph wire but also a new safety system for railway trains, in which a pilot drives a pilot engine one mile ahead of the train, but attached to it by a long wire. If the pilot engine has to stop for any reason, the governor stops rotating, shuts off the electric current, which has the effect of shutting off the steam supply to the main engine, and therefore stopping the train. But the most amazing idea he had was for what he called the electrochemical telegraph, and what we have come to call the fax machine.

He had already worked out how to set up a system of electric clocks that would keep exactly in time with one another. He put a master clock in the railway station in Edinburgh, and another clock in the railway station in Glasgow, each regulated by a pendulum. He arranged that every time the Edinburgh pendulum swung it sent a pulse along the telegraph wires, which drove a solenoid in Glasgow and kept the Glasgow pendulum exactly in time. This idea was crucial; it wasn't just that the clocks ran at the same rate – the electrical mechanism forced the pendulums to stay precisely in step. He then used the synchronised pendulums to drive the 'electrochemical telegraph'.

He made an etched copper positive of the page – text and/or picture – that he wanted to send, and mounted it beside the pendulum. Then he fixed an electrical stylus or brush on an arm so that as the pendulum swung it pushed the stylus to and fro across the page, making contact with the copper image. Thus each time the stylus came to a piece of copper, corresponding to a dark spot on the original image, a pulse was sent along the telegraph wires to the other end.

At the other end was a precisely matching arrangement, except that the receiving page was a sheet of electrosensitive paper. Whenever a pulse came along the telegraph wires, the stylus resting on the paper caused a black spot to appear, in a position corresponding to that of the black spot on the page being sent.

At both ends, Bain arranged that, after each complete swing of the pendulum, the pages dropped down by a small fixed amount – say one millimetre. So the sending picture was gradually scanned by the stylus, line by line, and every line was faithfully reproduced on the electrosensitive paper at the other end.

Unfortunately Bain was canny neither with his money nor about getting on with the Establishment. In 1840 he was desperate for financial support to develop his clocks and his fax machine; in an effort to help him, the editor of *Mechanics Magazine* introduced him to posh Professor Wheatstone, and Bain took his models to demonstrate at Wheatstone's house. After watching the demonstration with interest, Wheatstone said, 'Oh I shouldn't bother to develop these things any further; there's no future in them!' – but three months later demonstrated an electric clock to the Royal Society, claiming it was his own invention. Luckily, by then Bain had already applied for his patent.

Professor Sir Charles Wheatstone had all the advantages of rank and social position, and did his best to block Bain's patents. He failed, and when Wheatstone tried to get through an Act of Parliament to set up the Electric Telegraph Company, the House of Lords stepped in, called Bain as a witness, and eventually made the company pay Bain £10,000, and give him a job as manager. Wheatstone resigned in a huff.

Wheatstone is famous, Bain is forgotten. Sandy Bain,

despite his ingenuity, remained hopeless with money; he wasted a good deal on litigation in America, and much more in trying to achieve perpetual motion; he eventually died in Glasgow, poor and sad, in 1877. But the man who invented the fax machine, 120 years ahead of its time, was that unknown shepherd from Caithness, Alexander Bain.

The answering machine

Telephones were in common use in the 1880s, but the telephone answering machine feels like a thoroughly modern invention, scarcely needed until the busy office life of the 1980s demanded instant responses to every call. I was therefore surprised to discover that in 1899 Valdemar Poulsen of Copenhagen applied for a patent for 'Method of and Apparatus for Effecting the Storing Up of Speech or Signals by Magnetically Influencing

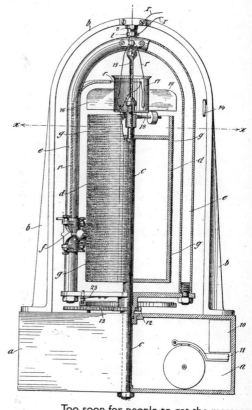

Too soon for people to get the message: Poulsen's answering machine (1899)

Magnetisable Bodies'. Essentially his apparatus was designed to record the incoming message magnetically on a coil of steel wire, and he claimed this would be 'of the greatest importance to the telephonic transmission of speech, as … communications transmitted in the absence of the subscriber at the receiving station, are directly received by the apparatus in order to be given out thereby to the subscriber whenever required'.

I am rather sad to think that, like Mr Bain, he cannot have made much money from his invention, because he was too far in advance of society.

Pneumatic tyres

The credit for inventing the first pneumatic tyre usually goes to the Scottish vet John Boyd Dunlop, who made some in 1888 for his son's tricycle. They were living in Belfast, and young Johnny complained that the cobbled streets made his bottom sore. Dunlop's tyres turned out to be not only comfortable but also fast; he persuaded the leading local cyclist Willie Hume to use them, and, when Hume won an important race at the Queen's College playing fields on 18 May 1889 (page 89), everyone else wanted pneumatic tyres too – and in due course the Dunlop Rubber Company was formed. However, Dunlop's were not the first pneumatic tyres, because 43 years earlier another Scot, Robert William Thomson, had patented and sold pneumatic tyres which he called 'elastic bearings' – but, alas, the world was not yet ready for them.

Born in Stonehaven in 1822, Robert Thomson was the eleventh child of the town's wealthy mill owner. He seems to have been a difficult child: because he hated school he was sent to America to learn to be a merchant, but he hated that too, so he came home again.

Not until his father gave him his own workshop when he was 17 did he find his true vocation as an engineer. He quickly made a name for himself with a handful of smart inventions – the ribbon saw, a clever rotary steam engine and the first electric detonator for firing mines, which impressed Michael Faraday. Like many engineers at the time he was soon caught up in the excitement of railways, and for some time worked with Robert Stephenson before setting up his own railway company.

At the age of 23, in 1845, he took out his first patent. He described his invention as 'the application of elastic bearings round the tyres of the wheels of carriages for the purpose of lessening the power required to draw the carriages, rendering their motion easier, and diminishing the noise they make when in motion' – in other words, pneumatic tyres.

Thomson made a tyre from a hollow belt of canvas, saturated on both sides with indiarubber or gutta-percha and cased in leather, and bolted it to the rim of the wheel. He inflated the tyres with air through a pipe 'fitted with an air-tight screw cap'. There is no mention of a valve, so the process of inflating the tyres must have been tricky. When inflated, his tyres were 5 inches (13 centimetres) thick.

The bicycle had scarcely been invented, and the motor car was far in the future; so Thomson's tyre was designed for horse-drawn carriages and especially steam carriages. Thomson wrote that:

> the comparatively small amount of power required to propel carriages, the wheels of which are fitted with these belts, the steadiness of the motion, the absence of all jolting and consequent security of the machinery from injury, the small damage the carriages will do to the roads, the absence of nearly all noise, the high speed that may be safely

> attained, and the great gentleness of the motion,
> will, I think, enable steam carriages to be run on
> common roads with great advantage both for
> carrying passengers and goods.

All such vehicles at that time had solid tyres, generally made of iron shrunk on to wooden wheels. These iron tyres were hard-wearing, which was important on the rough roads, and also were thought to be efficient; mechanics believed that a hard tyre resulted in low friction, in spite of the noise and discomfort.

But in 1847 Thomson proved that this was quite wrong, with a series of tests in London's Regent's Park. He took two noisy horse-drawn broughams, and fitted one with his elastic bearings. Then he measured the 'draught' – the effort required to pull each one over two different types of road, one rough and the other macadamised (that is, smooth).

The first thing that everyone noticed was that the carriage fitted with his tyres was silent, whereas iron tyres always made a loud grinding scrunching noise as they rolled along. His silent carriage caused quite a stir among the crowds in the park, and prompted lengthy discussions in *Mechanics Magazine*, who concluded:

> Despite the opinion most people would form ...
> that the draught must be greatly increased, [it] is
> unquestionably much lessened. The tyres are
> perfectly elastic as well as soft. They do not retard
> the carriage – they yield to every obstacle, permit
> the carriage to pass over it without rising up, and
> expanding as they pass from the obstruction, return
> the force borrowed for a moment to compress the
> tyre.

This description accurately describes the point of pneumatic tyres. When the wheel of a vehicle reaches an obstacle – say a stone in the path – it has to go over it. A wheel with a solid tyre can do this only by lifting into the air, which means lifting the whole vehicle into the air. This is noisy, uncomfortable and inefficient, since much of the energy of the horse is used in lifting the vehicle. A pneumatic tyre, by contrast, does not have to jump into the air: it merely squashes a little to allow the wheel to pass over the stone without jumping. The air in the tyre gets temporarily a bit more compressed, and so warms up a minute amount, but the ride is quiet, comfortable and efficient.

Thomson found in his tests that the 'draught' needed to pull the brougham was 60 per cent more for the solid tyres than the aerial wheels on the macadamised road, and three times as much on the rough road! As a result, great predictions were made about a revolution in transport, but although he steadily improved the design, introducing rivets for extra grip, rubber outer tyres, and puncture-proof inner tubes, he found great difficulty in getting hold of enough of the thin rubber sheets he needed, and eventually he was forced to abandon his idea.

Thomson carried on inventing – a self-filling fountain pen for the Great Exhibition in 1851, a portable steam crane in Java and solid rubber tyres for traction engines and road steamers. His rubber-tyred steam omnibus was immensely popular in Edinburgh. Perhaps his elastic bearings would have been a commercial success had the bicycle been invented earlier, but sadly for Thomson they were ahead of their time.

8 Flushed with failure

Flushing lavatories have been around for thousands of years – in his wonderful palace at Knossos on Crete, King Minos had flush-out lavatories with earthenware pans and wooden seats, and that was about 2000 BC. The Romans brought flushing toilets to Britain – you can still see the remains of a communal lavatory in the fort at Housesteads on Hadrian's Wall. However, the natives seem to have ignored this efficient sanitation, and as soon as the Romans left they went back to using holes in the ground.

Ajax

The first serious attempt we know about to invent a self-contained water closet was made by Sir John Harington, of Kelston Hall, near Bath. He was born in 1560, became a godson of Elizabeth I, and later achieved a reputation as a wit and a ladies' man at court. In 1598 he produced a book about a new kind of loo. The standard Elizabethan slang word for a lavatory or a privy was a Jakes; Harington jokingly called his book *The Metamorphosis of Ajax*, meaning the transformation of a lavatory. His book is full of such dreadful puns. He compares himself and his lavatory to Archimedes and his revelation in the bath, and he concludes with a practical section, on 'how unsaverie places may be made sweet, noysome places be made wholesome, filthie places made cleanly'.

A mock-up of Harington's self-contained water closet, Ajax (c. 1598)

The instructions say:

> In the Privie that annoys you, first cause a Cesterne
> ... to be placed either behind the seat, or in any
> place, either in the roome, or above it, from whence
> the water may by a small pype of lead of an inch
> [diameter] be convayed under the seat in the hinder
> part thereof (but quite out of sight) to which pype
> you must have a Cocke or washer [i.e. tap] to yeeld

> water with some pretie strength, when you would
> let it in.
>
> Next make a vessell of an oval forme, as broad at
> the bottome as at the top, ii foote deep, one foote
> broad, xvi inches long, place this verie close to your
> seate, like the pot of a close stool ... If water be
> plentie, the oftener it is used and opened, the
> sweeter; but if it be scant, once a day is inough, for
> a need, though twentie persons should use it.

The caption for the exploded diagram he provided said, 'This is Don Ajax house of the new fashion, all in sunder, that a workman may see what he hath to do.' The completed version, with fish in the cistern, was captioned 'Here is the same all put together that the workman may see if it be well.'

Ajax was meant to be left with six inches of water in the pan. To flush it, you unlocked the 'shell', unscrewed the bolt, and pulled it out to open the plug, which is at the bottom of the same rod. (The lock was to prevent 'children and busie folke' from wasting water.)

Sir John Harington was clearly an entertaining character, and his book shows not only that he thought a good deal about bodily functions in general and lavatories in particular, but also that he was not afraid to be explicit about them in writing. Most of this book would have been unprintable in Victorian times, and some of it raises eyebrows today.

Such a witty linguist and elegant ladies' man seems an unlikely candidate for engineer and plumber, but his servant M. Combe was certainly an artist, since he drew the pictures for the book, and probably a plumber too, for he wrote the practical section. Perhaps Combe was the designer, working to Harington's general brief.

Apparently Harington convinced the Queen, for she

allowed him to build an Ajax in her palace at Richmond, with a copy of the book chained to the wall beside it – but as far as we know this and his own were the only lavatories built to Harington's design; so Ajax was literally a wash out.

Slop closets

One of my favourite stories of lavatorial disasters is that of the grand communal-slop-closet experiment in Stafford in 1894. The automatic slop-water closet, or tipper closet, had a self-acting tipper. All the used bathwater and washing-up water in the house, and sometimes the rainwater off the roof, went not down the drain but into this tipper tank. When full, it overbalanced, and the soapy water rushed down a pipe and flushed the lavatory, which could be some distance away – for example in a privy out in the yard.

This was undoubtedly an economical and ecologically sound system, if only for the water saving, and also a tremendous advantage in the winter, for the privy did not have to have its own water supply, so it could not freeze up in cold weather. However, there was a snag: heavy rain made the cast-iron tippers discharge every few minutes, and their clanging all through the night could keep the whole family awake.

The idea of the tipper gradually spread throughout the world of sewage disposal. Roger George Salter took out a patent in 1848 that included the idea of putting tippers at intervals in sewers and drains so that water would collect until the 'self-acting flushing apparatus' tipped, on which 'the liquid rushes out with great velocity and force'.

Slop closets were in the 1890s seriously suggested as the best method of sanitation for households of the future.

In 1894 Staffordshire County Council instructed George Reid, the County Medical Officer, to set up a major experiment to test their efficiency, because they wanted 'to abolish the obnoxious privy-midden system … which then prevailed throughout the town, which … seriously endangered the public health'. So 59 houses, in two streets, were plumbed with slop closets. The sewage was all received in a well, large enough to contain a day's flow. From there at 7 o'clock every morning it was pumped into precipitation tanks, where they tried various types of filter and precipitant, none of which seemed to work very well.

'As regards the sewage itself,' Mr Reid wrote in his report, 'it is of the foulest description, indeed it far exceeds in foulness any sewage the analysis of which I have seen. Of course, considering the fact that it is composed solely of the slopwater of cottages and the excreta and urine of the inhabitants, one would naturally assume it to be fouler than would be the case had the closets in use been ordinary water-closets with a clean water flush. No doubt to a very large extent this is explained by the fact that the population contributing to the flow was entirely an artisan one …' Although I do not understand why Mr Reid should expect skilled workers to produce particularly foul sewage!

He concludes his report sadly:

> If then the Council determine to adhere to their intention of establishing the slop-closet system, it will, in my opinion, be necessary to … adopt a scheme of land filtration. The other alternative is to introduce ordinary water-closets in place of slop-closets … There are other objections, not least of which is the tendency to rapid putrefaction … That this has been the outcome of the experiments is disappointing, still it is better that the knowledge

should have been acquired now, before any harm has been done...

And so the communal slop closet generally faded from the scene, although a few were still in use in the 1980s, and children remember them because of the sudden spooky underground roar when the monsters flushed.

Valve closets

The first British patent for a water closet was taken out by a London watchmaker, Alexander Cumming, in 1775; his lavatory had a sliding valve underneath to let the sewage out. The problem with this was that it tended to get encrusted, and in winter to freeze up, especially if the closet was outside. Yorkshireman Joseph Bramah's splendid closet of 1778 overcame this problem by using a hinged valve.

Soon after this there appeared ingenious new closet ideas. Thomas Rowntree produced a portable water closet in 1789, and in 1792 John Ashley patented a self-acting water closet, 'which constantly keeps itself sweet and cleaner'. When the user stood up, an arrangement of wires and levers let the sewage out of the pan and then opened valves to flush the closet automatically. Thomas Binns's self-acting closet of 1793 was even more cunning. When you sat down the seat sank about a quarter of an inch, which was enough to activate a crank and a wire, and allow the 'measurer' to fill from the main cistern. When you stood up again the valve from the cistern was closed, and that below the measurer was opened, so that the water from the measurer flushed the lavatory. Binns was clearly an enterprising fellow, for he also invented various portable water closets.

In 1796 William Law patented a closet in which he

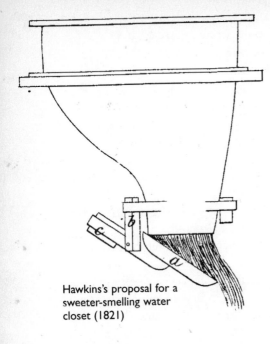

claimed 'Many Mechanical Gentlemen asert there are several Improvements … that have not been produced before … This Water Closet is principally intended to act by Riseing from the seat but may be acted by the handle …' Gradually the lavatories became more and more sophisticated;

Hawkins's proposal for a sweeter-smelling water closet (1821)

most of them seemed to have exotic refinements that have not stood the test of time.

In 1821 Stephen Hawkins produced a valve closet with a cunning air trap, designed to eliminate smells. When you used it, the weight of sewage falling on the trap *a* overcame the counterweight *c*, so that all the stuff fell through, and then the trap *a* closed again, and no smell could escape – at least in theory!

Before about 1850 only those people rich enough to have their own water supplies and cesspits were able to have water closets, but during the 1850s and 1860s piped water and sewers gradually reached most of the houses in Britain, and with these connections came the possibility of domestic water closets for the middle classes. Here was a market opportunity not to be missed, and sure enough inventors

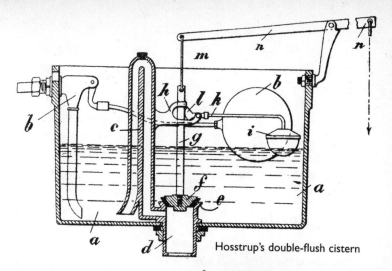

Hosstrup's double-flush cistern

queued for patents and vied with one another for the ingenuity of their systems.

By 1850 some 50 patents had been issued; by the end of 1855 there were more than a hundred, and after that the flood became a torrent. Many of these patents were for minor improvements in the flushing arrangements –

Crapper's ornamental flush-down W.C. (c. 1880)

Hans von Hosstrup, for example, invented 'a lever flushing-cistern in which an immediate flush is obtained by the pulling of the chain and an after flush is produced by the action of a syphon'; and Carl Nuber from Baden-Baden went to enormous lengths to make a powerful yet noiseless flushing system – but the fact is they were all failures, in that today's lavatories display little of the complex machinery that the Victorians were so fond of.

The urinette

Women have always been badly provided with public lavatories; even today in any public building there are almost always more loos for men than for women, even though women necessarily take longer for each visit. There used also to be the unfair fact that going into a cubicle cost a penny; hence the term spending a penny.

In 1927, concerned that women always had to pay to use a cubicle, while men could use urinals without charge, the Public Health Committee in London reported that 'a fitment for women has been designed, known as a urinette. It is similar to a w.c., but is narrower and has a flushing rim… Urinettes are fixed in w.c. compartments, usually with a curtain in front instead of a door.'

The idea was that, if a woman wanted only to wee, she could use the urinette for free, with modesty provided by a curtain; it was like a urinal for women.

Eight boroughs installed urinettes in a total of 30 places, but, the report confesses, 'The urinettes are not popular … the attendants state that they are sometimes used in an uncleanly manner and require supervision to maintain them in a hygienic condition.' And now, as far as I know, there are no urinettes to be found, although the idea was reinvented in 1999.

However, there was one great invention that failed undeservedly, in my view: the earth closet.

Earth closets

Before the advent of water closets, primitive lavatories were just holes in the ground. Dig out a pile of earth, go in the hole, and then shovel on a little earth to cover the offering. Earth closets became more advanced with the patent of Thomas Swinburne in 1838: he arranged a separate urinal for collecting urine, and a reservoir containing ashes, so that a small amount could be released after each use of the closet. In 1860 the Rev. Henry Moule entered the fray, patented his own closet, started the Moule Patent Earth Closet Company, and sold a range of models, the expensive ones made of oak or mahogany.

Basically the Moule system was to bring in earth from the garden, dry it in a metal box under the kitchen range and put it in a hopper at the back of the wooden closet, which was used indoors. After using it, you pulled a handle to 'flush' it with dry earth from the hopper; the earth covered your production, and according to Moule rapidly removed the smell. The earth could be redried and reused several times, and Moule claimed that he had no smells in the house, but a luxuriant growth of vegetables in his garden.

In 1861 he produced a 20-page pamphlet entitled *National health and wealth, instead of the disease, nuisance, expense, and waste, caused by cess-pools and water-drainage.* 'The cess-pool and privy vault are simply an unnatural abomination,' he thundered, 'the water-closet ... has only increased those evils.' The main environmental arguments are simple: first, every time you use a water closet you throw away up to 2 gallons (10 litres) of expensive drinking water; secondly you are also throwing away useful fertiliser;

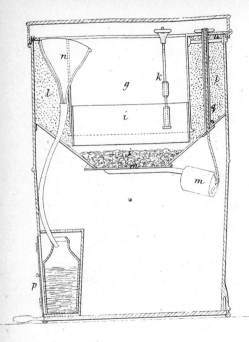

and thirdly the sewage has to decompose somewhere; underwater decomposition is slow and anaerobic, which means that it produces unpleasant smells and encourages potentially dangerous bacterial growth. Decomposition in dry earth, however, is aerobic and rapid; the sewage is quickly converted to harmless compost, and there is minimal smell.

Moule quoted a biblical precedent for his efforts, from a set of instructions about cleanliness: 'And thou shalt have a paddle upon thy weapon; and it shall be, when thou wilt ease thyself abroad, thou shalt dig therewith, and shalt turn back and cover that which cometh from thee.' (Deut. 23:13.) The New English Bible is even clearer: 'With your equipment you will have a trowel, and when you squat outside, you shall scrape a hole with it and then turn and cover your excrement.'

Henry Moule died in 1880, but even in his seventies he was still trying to persuade the government that the earth closet was the system of the future, and he managed to convince a lot of people. *The Lancet* of 1 August 1868 reported that 148 Moule dry-earth closets were used at the volunteer encampment at Wimbledon – forty or fifty of them daily by not fewer than 2,000 men – without the slightest annoyance to sight or smell. *The Field* of 21 November 1868, said 'In towns or villages not exceeding 2000 or 3000, we believe the earth-closet will be found not only more effective, but far more economical, than water drainage.'

Designs from Moule's Earth closet catalogue (1870)

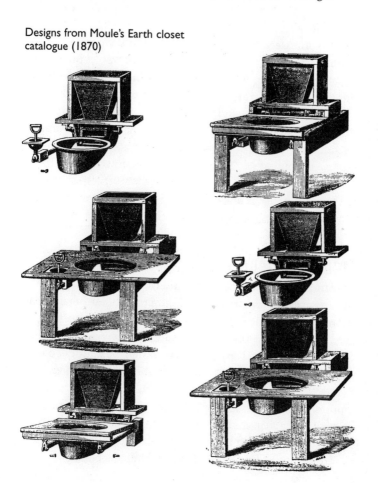

This combination of economy and health was powerful. In 1865 the Dorset County School at Dorchester, with 83 boys, changed from water closets to earth closets, and cut the annual maintenance costs from £3 to 10 shillings (50 pence)! At the same time smells and diarrhoea were eliminated. Lancaster Grammar School brought in earth closets because the water closets were always out of order 'by reason of marbles, Latin grammar covers, and other properties being thrown down them'.

For some decades in the second half of the nineteenth century, therefore, the earth closet and the water closet were in hot competition. Almost everything Moule said was true, and much the same arguments are used today by the champions of bioloos and composting lavatories; surely they represent our best hope for the future. The environmental considerations have not changed: using water closets is expensive, and merely shifts the problem downstream; the sewage has to decompose somewhere. Nevertheless in rich countries, because it does rapidly and effortlessly remove the sewage from the house, the water closet has won – so far.

Animal hygiene

An American book claims that any cat can be trained in 14 days to use an ordinary lavatory, and there have been many attempts to set aside special corners of parks for dog loos, mostly without conspicuous success, but two stories really caught my eye. An 1880 automatic stable was designed to allow horses and cows to walk on treadmills, and so do useful work, while at the same time collecting their own droppings, which could then be used directly as fertiliser.

I have not seen many of these automatic stables in use, but perhaps they will in any case be superseded by the Friendly Animal Trainer (FAT) recently developed by the

An automatic stable: enough to make a horse turn tail (1880)

Swiss Federal Station for Agricultural Economics and Engineering near Zürich. When a cow lifts its tail – as they do before performing – sensors warn the FAT, which lowers a pneumatically powered stirrup over the cow's neck and guides it to a 'toilet grill'. The sewage falls through on to a conveyor belt, and is taken away to generate methane, which heats the building. Meanwhile the rest of the floor stays clean.

Its inventor, Matthias Schick, claims that adult cows learn to use the machine in three weeks, but 'with young cows the process goes much faster. And you do not need to leave the trainer on all the time. You can use it one day and take it off the next.'

9 Brain-storms

Some inventions are purely practical, and lead to simple machines, but others are largely in the mind, and lead mainly to new ideas, or perhaps new ways of thinking about things. One of the most spectacular of these mental eureka! moments happened to a teenage teacher in a field in Doncaster.

A vision in Doncaster

George Boole was born in Lincoln, and became a precocious lad at school, translating Greek verse for fun. His dad was an incompetent shoemaker who went broke in the summer of 1831, and George, then only 15, had to go and look for a job to support the family. He couldn't find one in Lincoln, so he set off up the Great North Road, and walked 40 miles to Doncaster, where in South Parade he found a position as usher – junior teacher – in Mr Hyam's Academy, a strict school with high religious principles. They disapproved of young George: they suspected he read mathematics books on Sundays and, even worse, did sums in chapel!

The truth was he was miserable and lonely. He wrote home and complained that no one in Doncaster made gooseberry pies like his mum. He loved reading, but had no access to a library; so he had to buy books, and because he had so little money he chose books that took a long time to get through, because they represented good value. He found that maths textbooks were particularly hard going, and he bought several.

In his rare free time he liked to go walking, and luckily just across the road was a large patch of common land called Town Fields – even today it has several football fields and a lot of open space. One frosty day in January 1833 he was walking in Town Fields when he had what he described as a vision. He spoke about it often in later life, and said he felt like Saul on the road to Damascus. With his knowledge of mathematics, George knew that algebra could sort out most mechanical problems; his vision was that if you could dream up the right sort of algebra you could perhaps sort out mental problems – in other words unlock the secrets of the human mind!

George was eventually fired from the school in Doncaster, started his own school in Lincoln, and later became a professor in Ireland. He married Mary Everest, a niece of the colonel who surveyed India and gave his name to the world's highest mountain, and they had several children.

And his vision? Well, in a sense it was a failure, because George never did unlock the secrets of the human mind, but in another sense it was a triumph, because after working on his idea for many years he wrote a book called *The Laws of Thought*, in which he developed a new system of logic that came to be called, in his honour, Boolean algebra. This was of considerable interest at the time, but the real pay-off came a hundred years later, when Claude Shannon and the other people making the first computers realised that George Boole's algebra could be used to make simple electrical switches perform complicated logical calculations. And today, inside every computer, word processor, and even calculator, there are circuits that depend entirely on Boolean algebra – stemming from that vision in a field in Doncaster.

The first mechanical computer?

Some years before George Boole was dreaming away in Doncaster, an irascible busker-hater was trying to build a calculating machine in London. Born on Boxing Day 1791, Charles Babbage was found by a fellow student at Cambridge sitting lost in deep thought over a book of logarithms. When asked what he was thinking about he said he had had this amazing idea: logs could be calculated by machine, and then there wouldn't be mistakes in them.

He became popular in London society, and in 1816 was elected a Fellow of the Royal Society. He soon began pursuing his idea of a mechanical calculator, and by 1820 had built a small model to show the Royal Society, who were impressed by the scheme, and gave it their blessing. Babbage then went to the government to ask for financial backing, and succeeded in persuading the Chancellor of the Exchequer to promise him £1,500. Unfortunately this meeting was informal, and no notes were taken. Babbage came away thinking the £1,500 was just an advance, whereas the Chancellor thought it was the complete amount. However, at least Babbage was able to make a start, and he hired Joseph Clement, a skilled engineer from the stable of Henry Maudslay, to build his Difference Engine, working from his home in Southwark.

The Difference Engine was designed to carry out routine calculations, to find square roots and logarithms, for example, using what is called the method of differences, which allows complex calculations to be carried out in a large number of simple steps of addition and subtraction. Since every step was to be done by machine, no errors could creep in; it was a lovely idea. All the machine would do was add and subtract, using as a guide the number of teeth on the cogwheels, so that it could not make a mistake.

In 1828, after a long trip abroad, Babbage returned to

that great poet, romantic and seducer of women George Gordon, Lord Byron. When she was only four months old, Ada's parents had a noisy divorce, and she never saw her father again, although he wrote about her in *Childe Harold:*

> *Is thy face like thy mother's, my fair child*
> *Ada, sole daughter of my house and of my heart?*
> *When last I saw thy young blue eyes they smiled,*
> *And then we parted – not as now we part,*
> *But with a hope.*

Ada became a mathematician, and in 1833 – the same year as George Boole's vision – she met Charles Babbage, and became fascinated by his dreams of calculating engines. He never wrote anything useful about them, and the best information we have about the potential of his Analytical Engine comes from her notes. She explained how it would have taken instructions on punched cards, in what we now call a program. She described the 'store' or memory, and the 'mill' or central processing unit, and she speculated about what the machine might be capable of: it would not produce original ideas, but it would greatly help the advance of science, and it might be helpful in composing music, she thought. She clearly had a vision of the future, and would have loved the computers of today.

She also described in detail exactly what instructions it would need to perform a number of complex mathematical calculations. We don't know how much of this was her work, and how much Babbage's, but she was certainly the first person to write it down, and she can therefore reasonably be described as the world's first computer programmer! Indeed, the programming language 'Ada' was named after her.

Ada had tremendous ambition. She believed she would

be able to work out the mathematics of the brain; I can't help wondering whether she had heard of Boole's ideas! At one point Ada wrote to Babbage, 'The more I study, the more irresistible do I feel my genius to be.' But her life was tragic, she died from cancer at the age of 36, and the Analytical Engine never existed except in Babbage's mind and her notes.

A sensible calendar

Moses Bruine Cotsworth was born near York in 1859, and spent most of his life working for the railway, not with the trains and the track and so on, but with figures. He was obsessed by numbers, and he was a statistician – but his real passion was for reform of the calendar. The essence of Cotsworth's system was simple: he described it in his curious book *The Rational Almanac*, which is unusually tall and narrow. He said it was pocket-size; I guess he must have had very long pockets!

All the information you need to understand his calendar is in a table on the inside of the front cover, but he actually wrote 471 more pages to justify his claims and assertions. The reason he waxed so passionate about reforming the calendar is that the existing one is so absurd. Have a look at the year 2000; the first day of the year is a Saturday; 1 February is a Tuesday; 1 March is a Wednesday. In Cotsworth's system, much simpler, the first of January is a Sunday, the first of February is a Sunday, the first of March is a Sunday, and the first of every month is a Sunday, because every month is 28 days long. There are 365 days in a year, and 365 divided by 28 equals 13 (with one day over); so he needed 13 months. Therefore he invented another month, the month of the sun; he called it Sol, and he put it between June and July.

Because 13 x 28 makes 364, 13 months of 28 days leave just one spare day. In Cotsworths's system the extra day became Christmas Day. After Sunday the 22nd of December came Christmas Day, which was not a day of the week. Then he went on with Monday the 23rd, and the year ended as usual on the 28th of the month. He accommodated leap years in the same way, by simply putting in an extra day, but not counting it as a day of the week. The whole system was highly logical, and would certainly have made life simpler; we should scarcely have needed diaries and year planners if every month always began on a Sunday.

The sad thing is that Cotsworth's brilliant scheme failed, because he failed to persuade everyone to take it up, even though he was on the League of Nations Calendar Reform Committee. One person he did persuade was George Eastman, who ran the Kodak Company, and, until a few years ago, every Kodak employee was paid in 13 monthly instalments.

10 Domestic difficulties

The Victorian age of sophistication brought with it a number of obsessions, among which was the idea of constantly improving both yourself and your household. Somewhere near the heart of their worries lay the dreadful problem of personal hygiene.

Keeping clean

A Scarborough ironmonger, Alfred Wrightson, invented a cunning wire soap holder that would hang over the edge of the bath – or a pail or bowl – to hold the soap out of the water.

Edmund Roenius of Grand Rapids in Michigan was more ambitious with his soap hanger: he wanted to make sure the

Wrightson's 'Improved Soap Holder' (1899)

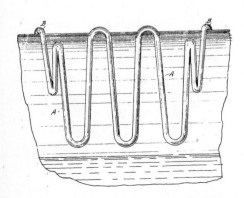 

soap could not fall to the
ground or be carried away.
The cake of soap was
moulded round a metal
tube so that it could not
be removed. It was then
suspended on a chain
which passed over a
pulley on a bracket, and
had a counterweight at the
other end. The soap
hanger was mounted on
the wall. 'The soap is thus
prevented from collecting
dirt through contact with
a soap dish, washstand, or
other supporting surface,
and it cannot slip from the
hands of the user and fall
on the floor. The device
also effects a saving of
soap and prevents the same from being lost or carried
away.'

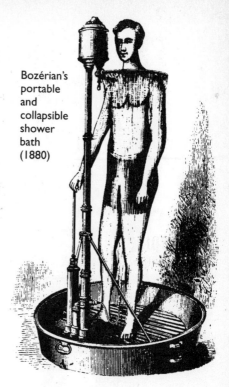

Bozérian's
portable
and
collapsible
shower
bath
(1880)

In 1880 Gaston Bozérian devised a handy portable and
collapsible shower bath, in which the water was pumped up
by hand to a small overhead reservoir. In 1897 the Parisians
attending the Bicycle Exhibition were amazed to see the
Vélo-douche, or bicycle shower. They suggested that the user
could keep in training while washing, and one great
advantage of the system was that, the harder you pedalled,
the more powerful was the flow of water. A heater below
the water tank would allow you to have a hot shower.
Confident predictions were made that these *Vélo-douches*
would become commonplace in cycling clubs and schools.
In both these showers, the water seems to have been

recycled; so it must have become gradually fairly soapy and grubby.

... and keeping fit

During the early eighteenth century, the Guppy family were a significant force in Bristol society. Thomas Guppy was an iron founder, and more than that a merchant venturer. He it was who invited Isambard Kingdom Brunel, impressed by his designs for the Clifton Suspension Bridge, to think about building a railway from Bristol to London (not from London to Bristol!). Tom Guppy became a close associate and even friend of Brunel, and worked with him on many projects. After a tremendous lunch at Taplow to celebrate the opening of the Great Western Railway, he walked along the top of the moving train as it steamed back towards Paddington, and twenty years later he cast the vital iron pipes for Brunel's ill-fated atmospheric railway (see pages 33-7).

Tom's brother Samuel Guppy was a successful merchant in Bristol, with posh premises in Queens' Square; he took out patents for improvements in the manufacture of nails and soap. Sam's wife Sarah Guppy must have been intrigued by these patents, and decided to take out some of her own. In 1831 she patented an ingenious bedstead with special steps which slid under each side to prevent dust from gathering under the bed, as well as making it easier to get into and out of the bed. The bed was also fitted with 'a set of springs and rollers to be used for exercise when in bed'. In other words her bed made it possible to do pull-ups without even getting up first!

Kitchen capers

However, my favourite Sarah Guppy patent was taken out in 1812, for 'Certain improvements in tea and coffee urns'. She says she made her tea urn in any of the 'usual forms and constructions', but it had two clever modifications, in order to allow the user to make the whole of breakfast in one operation, instead of having to mess about with several different pieces of equipment. First she suspended an egg basket from the lid, so that the eggs in the basket hung in the water, and were boiled while the water was boiling to make the tea. And second, in the lid of the urn, she made 'an elegant and convenient support for a plate or dish or other vessel to contain toast or other article of food or refreshment' – in other words, a place to keep the toast warm. Why every modern kitchen is not equipped with one of Sarah's tea urns must remain a mystery.

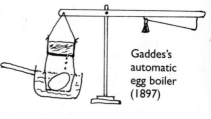

Gaddes's automatic egg boiler (1897)

Egg-boiling equipment has always been a favourite goal for inventors, and one of the more splendid examples of the genre was the automatic egg boiler patented by Dr Thomas Gaddes, a dentist in Harrogate. Actually there was not much automatic about the boiling process, but he devised a cunning way of snatching the egg from the boiling water at the right moment. Perhaps he was kept so busy by agonised patients demanding to have their teeth treated that he was unable to time his egg with a watch or even an hourglass egg timer, or perhaps he was just absent-minded, and wandered off, allowing his eggs to become hard as rocks.

The Gaddes machine depended on water dripping from a reservoir, which therefore gradually became lighter and allowed the balance arm to tilt. This would have lifted the egg slowly from the water, but Gaddes realised that this might have left the egg hard underneath and soft on top, so

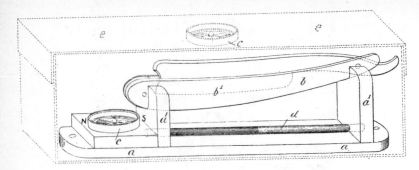

D'Oyley Grange's knife and razor stand (1899)

he added a clever refinement in the shape of a fishing
weight on a separate wire slide. As soon as this slide dipped
below the horizontal, the weight slid to the other end of the
wire, the balance of the arm was suddenly shifted and the
egg was yanked from the water. The wire slide could be
adjusted for large, medium or small eggs, and there was
even a modification to allow two eggs to be boiled at the
same time.

Harrogate must have been a town of ingenious chefs, for
William D'Oyly Grange of Clarence Drive patented a special
stand for holding knives and razors, in order to keep them
sharp by means of a magnetic field. The knife or razor was
placed in a box with the edge down and the whole of the
blade at an angle of 15 degrees to the horizontal. Attached
to the box was a compass to permit the box 'being placed in
a particular position in relation to the magnetic field of the
earth. At one end of the box ... is placed a weak magnet or
as an alternative the compass. If a magnet it is to be
removable. In using this appliance I take the magnet out and
place the empty case or stand in a drawer or on a wooden
shelf or other suitable place and turn the box until the north
end of the needle points to an arrow on the stand or box.'
He says that the knife or razor should always be left in a

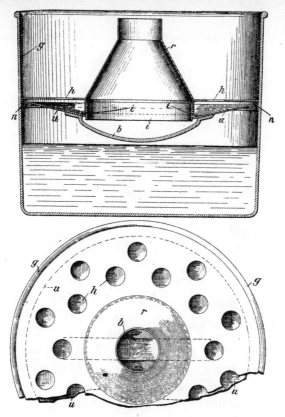

Krogh's milk boiler (1899)

north–south line, in order to keep the edge sharp!

Marius Frederik Krogh developed a complex-looking piece of apparatus to prevent milk boiling over. When you put this into the saucepan the whole device sank directly on to the level of the milk and, 'yielding gradually to the pressure of the boiling milk, prevented the boiling over of the latter ...' If the milk boiled too soon, it went up through the central funnel, spilled over, cooling, and ran back down through the perforations into the body of the liquid. 'The

Kürten's candle stove (1899)

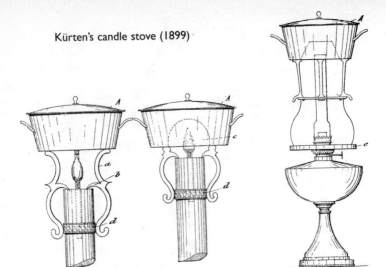

action of this apparatus is found to be excellent, one of the principal features being that the device can rise and fall ... according to as the milk boils more or less.'

Hubert Caspar Kürten of Switzerland invented a clever little clip to fit on a candle so that it could be used for cooking. The saucepan could have a flat bottom or a concave bottom (for more efficient heat transfer), and the three legs of the stand hung on the candle so that it descended as the candle burned. The saucepan remained at the same height above the flame. This looks as though it would be useful for making a cup of tea,

Heated flower stand (1899)

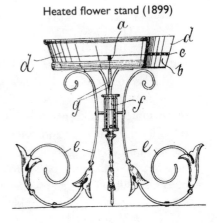

although candle flames are rather sooty, as I remember from trying to use them for illegal toast production at school.

On the other hand Marie Deutschmann's invention of a heated flower stand seems absurd. She says its object is to improve and accelerate the growth of the flowers placed inside it, but it seems to me that the heat from the spirit lamp she suggests would be enough to cook them!

From the cradle to the grave

Another great preoccupation of the Victorians was cradle rocking. Some parents – or perhaps nurses – seem to have thought that no baby could possibly get to sleep without being rocked in its cradle, and no doubt the gentle motion

A cradle-rocking machine (1873)

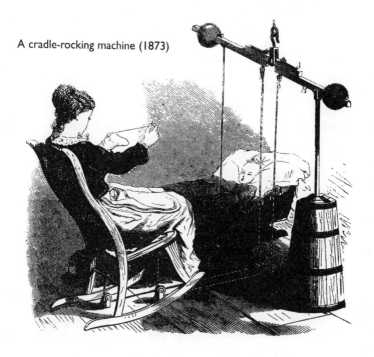

had a soporific effect. As a lad in the early 1800s Thomas Edmondson, who in later life made a small fortune from his brilliant idea of the locally printed railway ticket, complete with number and date stamp, built a combined cradle rocker and butter churn, so that anyone who was churning the butter would simultaneously rock the baby.

This sounds quite tough to me – churning the butter must be hard enough already, without having to rock the baby as well. What's more, I should have thought that butter churning must involve movements that are much quicker and more violent than would be ideal for baby rocking …

However, this did not prevent the same idea being reinvented in America in 1873. I guess a man claimed credit for this invention, for he suggested it would employ 'the hitherto wasted female power' to rock the baby and make the butter. 'By this means,' he went on, 'the hands of the fair operator are left free for darning stockings, sewing, or other light work … Fathers of large families of girls … are thus afforded an effective method of diverting the latent feminine energy, usually manifested in the pursuit of novels, beaux, embroidery, opera-boxes, and bonnets, into channels of useful and profitable labour.' He even suggests that the device could 'supply power for washing machines, wringers, and other articles of household use'. This man would not be popular if he made such suggestions today – indeed I don't expect he was popular with women in 1873!

I am sure that many other cradle rockers were invented, but one that was actually patented in 1899 by a Canadian called Lewis Cutten of the County of Turtle Mountain, was constructed rather like a grandfather clock: wind up the clock spring and let go. The cradle is driven one way by the spring, and then swings back under gravity, before being pushed again. All you need to try it out is an old grandfather clock and a baby!

One of the more flamboyant characters of the Industrial Revolution was John 'Iron-mad' Wilkinson, who was born on a market cart headed for Workington Fair, became an ironmaster in the West Midlands, and wanted to make everything from iron. He built an iron boat, which everyone else wrongly predicted would sink. He built an iron church, with iron pews and iron pulpit, now carefully painted to look like wood. He was involved in 1779 in the casting of the famous iron bridge, which spans the Severn and gave its name to the developing town there. And he cast himself an iron coffin, which he stood in the corner of his office and showed off proudly to all his visitors.

When he died in 1808 his body was placed in a wooden coffin and taken to the planned burial site at Castle Head, but unfortunately the wooden coffin was too big to fit into his iron coffin; so they buried him temporarily in the garden while a new coffin was cast. Then they dug him up, put the wooden coffin in the new iron coffin, and found that it was now too big for the hole in the rock. So they buried him temporarily again, blasted a bigger hole in the rock, and dug him up and buried him properly, with a huge iron obelisk above him. However, 20 years later the house changed hands, and the new owners objected to having this iron obelisk outside their windows; so poor Iron-mad was dug up for the third time and buried for the fourth time, at Lindale church.

A final twist: he had been so popular with his workers that, seven years after his death, several thousand of them gathered on Monmore Green and sang for him, hoping that he would reappear on his grey horse, and lead them back to prosperity after the misery of the Napoleonic Wars. But it was all in vain – he stayed in his iron coffin.

Matches and sticks

One small difficulty that has beset people for a long time is that it takes two hands to light a match, which means that you lack a hand to hold the candle, lamp, cigar or whatever it is you need to light. I once met a pipe-smoking Jaguar driver, who after years of practice had perfected a way of taking a Swan Vesta from the box and striking it with one hand, so that he could light his pipe with one hand on the wheel. I greatly admired his prestidigitatory skill, but never mustered the time, patience and dexterity needed to do it for myself.

An elegant solution to the two-hand-match problem came from George Frederick Lawrence and Arthur Josiah Field, whose object was 'to produce a holder or box from which a match can be taken and through which when passing it can be automatically lighted, and held still burning for igniting a cycle lamp, pipe, cigar, or other article'.

Their claim continues: 'We make our holder in the form of a metal case in which we place a slide … having at one end flexible springing jaws on which are attached roughened or serrated lips for the match to pass through and be ignited. We arrange a pusher … for the purpose of ejecting the match … and for forcing it through the igniting jaws.' So the match was pushed between the sandpapery jaws and ignited as it emerged. They also allowed for it to be flipped through with a spring when released by a trigger, which would have been dramatic. In either case the device must have made it easy to light a match with one hand.

A hi-tech version of automatic ignition was provided in France by Monsieur Delostal; it looked like a bell and was called the electric match. The match is the stick in the middle, A, and has at its further end a hollow perforated space filled with cotton. When inserted into the bell this cotton soaks up flammable liquid from the reservoir E at the bottom, which is filled with felt saturated with a mixture of alcohol and ether. The instrument is connected to an electric battery by means of two wires. As the stick A is pulled out, it breaks an electrical contact with the small watch spring D. This causes an electric spark, which ignites the end of the match. *Eh voilà; le feu!* After use, the match is replaced in the bell, and the absence of air inside extinguishes the flame. *C'est magnifique, n'est-ce pas?*

The modern corollary to these autostrike matches is threefold. First we have gas or petrol lighters, which need only one hand. Second we have flint or electronic spark

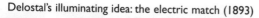

Delostal's illuminating idea: the electric match (1893)

generators to light gas rings – rather as Monsieur Delostal had – and most gas cookers and central-heating boilers are fitted with automatic spark lighting, so that the gas cannot be turned on and left running. Third, many of us still use the simple match, as invented by John Walker in 1826.

Joseph Emmett was perhaps concerned about the number of cases of walking-stick-user's wrist in the community of East Dulwich when he patented his improved rubber-tipped ferrule for walking sticks, umbrellas, billiard cues and the like. He provided a metallic ferrule or collar, preferably conical, with both ends open, and placed a plug of indiarubber in the bottom, sticking out through the bottom of the cone. The other end fitted on the walking stick or umbrella, and was attached in the usual way. Emmett claimed that:

> **By this invention, the objectionable noise & concussion of the ordinary solid-tipped ferrule is entirely done away with; as likewise is the very sensible shock to the hand & arm felt at every impact between the ordinary solid-tipped ferrule & the hard pavement or road. The comfort of the user is largely increased by the interposition of the soft and yielding material especially in the case of aged and infirm persons.**

Domestic animals

William H. Wellstead, a farmer from Michigan, invented a clever system for feeding cows, which aimed 'to regulate the supply of feed to an animal so as to prevent too rapid eating, insufficient mastication, and waste of feed'. The feeding trough could move vertically up and down, and was supported by an adjustable weighted lever, so that when the cow pressed with its nose on the trough a limited amount of grain or other feed would fall into the trough, and when the pressure of the nose was removed, the flow of grain stopped.

He claimed that:

> **The animal is thus prevented from eating too rapidly and is compelled to masticate and digest its feed more thoroughly, thereby enabling it to assimilate a larger percentage of its feed and to be kept in a better and healthier condition with less feed than when the usual methods and appliances are employed. The waste that occurs from scattering, slobbering or moistening with saliva what is not eaten, when a considerable quantity of grain or feed is given to the animal at once, in the usual way of feeding, is prevented, and the disorders of the alimentary canal resulting from improper eating are also avoided.**

This limited supply of food seems quite sensible, although why it should force the animal to chew more thoroughly is not clear. I wonder whether the continued use of such a device would in time produce a race of supercows which would pick up a brick and dump it in the trough in order to release all the feed in the hopper!

Partly for the benefit of the horse, because the work would be easier, Giuseppe Vicenzo de Luca took out a patent for a new lightweight plough, intended to be used in market gardens. The main innovation was a revolving ploughshare, which he asserted would be just the thing for the cultivation of light soils.

March 1879 saw the dawning of a new age in New York bird care, for Owen W. Taft received a patent for a collapsible bird cage, or as he put it 'a bird cage adapted

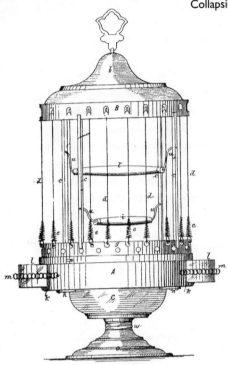

primarily to being taken to pieces and packed in smaller compass for facility of transportation, and constructed so that it is held in its complete integral form by a tension exerted either individually or collectively upon the several wires constituting the same'.

I assume the point of having a collapsible bird cage was that it was easy to take to the country for the weekend, or to Long Island for a vacation, but what Mr Taft fails to explain in his long and complex patent is what you were supposed to do with the poor inhabitant when the cage was collapsed. Did you have to have a collapsible bird as well?

11 Medical marvels

People have always disliked being ill, and much human time and energy have been devoted to gadgets and tinctures intended to improve the sense of well being; that is to make people who are ill – or think they are ill – feel better. There must have been many more remedies proposed than there are diseases to treat, from the proverbial snake oil of the charlatan pedlars of the Wild West to the soothsayer's charms that were supposed to dispose of warts. Here are just a few of the more bizarre ideas.

Pneumatic medicine

During the seventeenth and eighteenth centuries, 'taking the waters' was a fashionable way for people who felt generally unwell to treat themselves, and one of the popular resorts was Hotwells Spa at Bristol, where hot murky water gushed out from St Vincent's Rock, roughly underneath where the Clifton Suspension Bridge now stands. Catherine of Braganza visited Hotwells in 1677, and that really put the place on the map. Many of

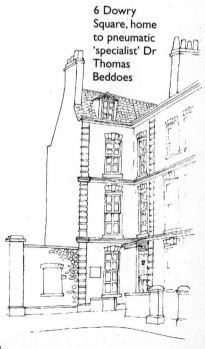

6 Dowry Square, home to pneumatic 'specialist' Dr Thomas Beddoes

the people who came lodged down the road in elegant Dowry Square, and at No. 6 Dr Thomas Beddoes set up in October 1798 his brand-new Pneumatic Institution, hoping to cash in on all these sick visitors. As medical superintendent he hired the 19-year-old Humphry Davy.

The Pneumatic Institution was funded by private subscription – they had £1,500 from the potter Josiah Wedgwood, for example – and its aim was to find out whether the various gases that had recently been discovered by Priestley, Lavoisier and others had any useful medicinal value. The institution took eight inpatients and up to 80 outpatients, many of whom had tuberculosis, which was common at the time, and deadly. Because tuberculosis clearly affected the breathing system, Beddoes hoped that some form of gas therapy would be effective; he and Davy tried all sorts of gases.

Beddoes apparently believed that cows were healthy beasts, and therefore that patients with tuberculosis might be cured by the gases produced by cows. As far as we know he did not actually take cows into the ward, but he kept a small herd in the garden next door, and piped the gases into the bedchambers. These gases, you understand, were what the cows breathed out, and what came from the other end as well … There is no evidence that this weird treatment did the patients any good at all, but I imagine there was quite an incentive to feel better and discharge yourself!

However, this curious obsession with gases did have one useful side effect, for Davy discovered the wonderful effects of inhaling nitrous oxide,

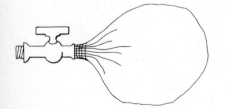

Not all for laughs: Davy's trick of inhaling nitrous oxide became a great success with medics (1799)

which came to be called laughing gas. He used to wander round the Downs, breathing it from a green silk bag, and he introduced the practice to his friends. The poet Robert Southey wrote to his brother, 'O Tom! Such gas has Davy discovered ... it made me laugh and tingle in every toe and fingertip. Davy has actually invented a new pleasure for which language has no name!'

Today, nitrous oxide is used not so much by poets as by dentists, nurses and paramedics, for it is one of the most safe and useful of the anaesthetics; but it all started with Beddoes's theory about cows!

In 1876 Dr Carlo Forlianini opened an elegant Pneumatic Health Institute in Milan. The patient was taken into a cylindrical, comfortably furnished room (see below) into

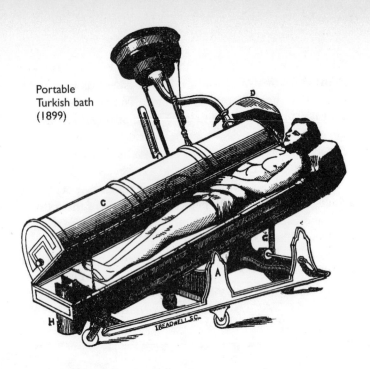

Portable
Turkish bath
(1899)

which chemically purified air was blown at high pressure,
using a steam engine. Dr Forlianini's theory was that the
extra pressure forced the clean air into the tiniest tubules in
the lungs, which improved the oxygenation of the blood,
swept away any particles or impurities and strengthened the
breathing muscles, bringing great benefits to those suffering
from diseases of the blood, pulmonary or glandular systems.

The Turkish bath was all the rage in the late nineteenth
century, but some people worried that, although the hot air
was clearly beneficial to the skin and the body in general, it
might perhaps be injurious to the lungs. So in 1873 the
British Medical Journal announced to the world a new,
improved, portable Turkish bath, which was designed to fit
closely around the body, leaving the head free in order to
spare the lungs. This apparatus was adjustable in every way,

and even had an attached cistern to provide the patient with a warm or cool shower, either slowly or rapidly. I am intrigued by the fact that this was clearly perceived as a medical treatment, and suggested by the *British Medical Journal* for the use of patients, whereas today Turkish baths are generally thought of as recreational.

A London mining agent, Arthur Lewis Pointing, patented an improved folding cabinet for vapour and hot-air baths, which was cheap and simple and so brought the portable Turkish bath within the range of ordinary people. Imagine a box about four feet (1.2 metres) in each dimension, the walls and lid being made of waterproof fabric on wooden frames. You sit inside this box on a chair, with your head poking out through a little hole in the roof, fitted with its own box, which can be thrown back to allow the user to breathe cool air. However, I believe the point was to fill the entire cabinet with steam, hot air or balsamic vapours, to ease the breathing system. And the beauty of the cabinet was that it would fold completely flat for easy storage!

The Quaker bath

A popular American accessory was the Quaker steam or vapour bath, which was a cylinder of fabric, and cost only $5 by

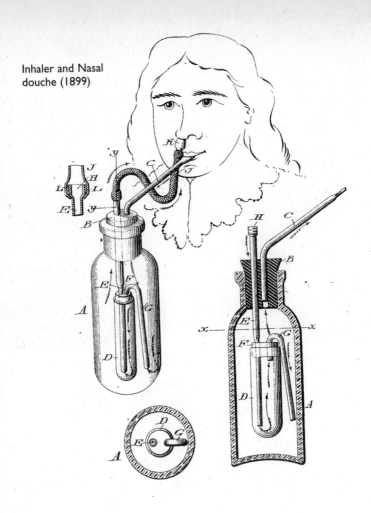

Inhaler and Nasal
douche (1899)

mail order. Steam for these portable baths could be provided
from the kitchen kettle, or from a metal bowl of water into
which was put a brick heated in the fire. Hot air was
provided by a small spirit lamp.

Inhalation of beneficial vapours was widely used to treat
all sorts of illnesses, real or imagined, and dozens of devices

Taking the air or putting the kettle on? A home-made inhaler (1894)

were dreamed up to assist in the process. James Monroe Munyon from Philadelphia patented a simple but ingenious combined inhaler and nasal douche. Either the vapour from medicament contained within the small vessel D could simply be inhaled through the mouthpiece, or the nosepiece K could be fitted, and the patient could blow into the mouthpiece to squirt the vapour up his nose – although blowing out through the mouth and breathing in through the nose might be a bit tricky.

Some patients have always believed in do-it-yourself medicine, as shown by the home-made inhalation equipment of 1894 (above).

A Manchester printer-turned-doctor, Charles Blackley, suffered dreadfully from hay fever, and was prompted to investigate what caused it in the spring of 1859, when his children brought some grasses into the house and set off the familiar symptoms much earlier than June, when he expected them. Some people said hay fever was caused by the smell of roses, others by dust, paint or varnish fumes, or even sunlight. He tried all these things on himself, and found that the only substance that caused real runny-eyed, snotty-nosed, phlegm-chested hay fever was pollen from grasses and flowers.

Charles Blackley never got as far as finding a cure for hay fever, but he suggested various ways of avoiding it, including muslin nose plugs to filter out the pollen. Unfortunately they proved awkward to use, and made breathing difficult, and they never caught on.

A Hungarian glass painter, Carl Kusché, invented an improved spittoon 'having a floating surface to receive the expectoration, said surface being capable of being depressed by the foot below the level of the water or other disinfected liquid in which it floats, and thus to wash off the impurities from the same'.

Encouraged perhaps by the acute hearing of elephants, Shamrao Babajee Powar of Bombay patented a neat piece of apparatus to assist hearing (opposite). It comprised a pair of bent or hollowed plates of aluminium or celluloid, rather like convoluted sea shells. These fitted over and around the ears, leaving openings in front which had an area greater than that of the ears, thus forming a chamber to receive the sound waves on its inner surface and reflect them into the ear cavity. These plates could be held in place either by a light spring frame fitting over the top of the head, or by being attached to a handle held below the chin.

I am reminded of the Rev. John Blackburn of Sheffield, who was worried that some of his congregation might not be able to hear the golden words of his sermons; so he constructed a parabolic reflector above and behind his pulpit in order to project his message more effectively into the church. History does not relate whether this worked, but I am a bit worried that, if his reflector was truly parabolic, his thundering tones

Powar's Improved Hearing Device (1899)

would all either go forth in a narrow parallel beam, or else, even worse, be focused on a single pew some distance in front of him, in which case one loyal churchgoer might be deafened, while all the rest of the congregation would be worse off than before!

Henry Tansley, gentleman of Brighton, was unhappy about conventional spectacle frames (see over) that hooked on to the ears. He does not reveal why this was the case – perhaps they made his ears sore. In any case, he patented a new design for spectacle frames, with shorter arms that ended in forks. The ends of these forks were to be provided with rounded serrated ends so that they would rest comfortably on the temples or cheek bones, and the glasses would be kept in place by a string behind the head.

In 1793 John Dalton, the new Professor of Mathematics and Natural Philosophy at the New College in Manchester, scientifically described colour-blindness for the first time. He himself was unable to tell the difference between red and green, which we now call red-green deficient, and he elegantly described his own observations of the condition.

He realised that colour-blindness must be hereditary, since his brother saw things the same way as he did.

After thinking about his colour-blindness for years, Dalton became convinced that he could not distinguish between red and green because his eyeballs were tinted blue, and in a rather macabre way asked that after his death his eyes should be removed so that his theory could be proved. When he died in 1844, his body was placed in Manchester Town Hall, and 40,000 people filed past to pay their last respects. But he was wrong about his eyeballs: when they were removed they turned out not to be tinged at all. We now know colour-blindness is caused by a missing gene. However, for many years it was called Daltonism, after him.

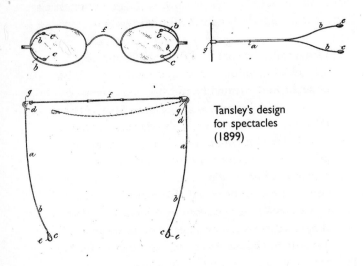

Tansley's design
for spectacles
(1899)

12 Fun and games

The Victorians seem to have taken everything rather seriously, even themselves. Life should be regular and organised, and even their games had to be played by the book. As a result they took out many patents for toys and games, and even some for crackers!

An electrical engineer called James Ernest Spagnoletti, of Ealing, must have been dissatisfied with conventional Christmas crackers, since he invented a new type:

> **I form my improved cracker, of any suitable material, in the form of what is known as a 'wish bone' or in the form of an horse shoe, one side or arm of which is weakened at any desired spot; to the other side or arm of the 'wish bone' or horse shoe I attach, in any desired manner, the usual prize or gift which is suitably enclosed. The explosive or detonating material is contained in a strip of paper or other suitable material connected to each side or arm of the 'wish bone' or horse shoe, so that when the sides or arms are pulled in opposite directions, fracturing said paper or other connection, a report will take place ...**

Actually I like the idea of combining the festive Christmas cracker with the old folklore idea that wishbones and horseshoes bring luck, so I am sorry that these new

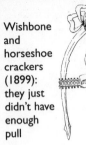

Wishbone and horseshoe crackers (1899): they just didn't have enough pull

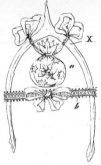

Design for a Victorian toy: the double hoop with windmills (1899)

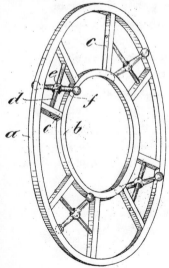

improved crackers failed to take over the Christmas table. On the other hand I disapprove strongly of the designated weak spot, which is presumably built in so that a generous parent can make sure that the child at the other end gets all the 'luck' – or conversely so that greedy pigs can scoop all the prizes for themselves. What Mr Spagnoletti does not mention is the dreadful jokes; perhaps they were a later invention.

In Kattowitz, Silesia, in the German Empire, Joseph Reidel and Rudolph Block produced a complex variation of the hoop, that quintessential Victorian toy. Their new hoop had a second hoop inside it, and a clever arrangement of little windmills, each of a spindle with two arms ending in a cup or an angled blade, so that when the hoop was bowled along the ground, the arms would spin in the slipstream.

When I first saw the diagram for Henry Long's rowing boat I thought it was meant to be one of those fiendish exercise machines in which you are supposed to row furiously without getting anywhere. However, it turned out to be a simple toy. When you pull it along the table or the floor the chap inside appears to be rowing. He is in fact supported on a pivot, and is made to rock to and fro by a lever attached to a crank on one of the wheels. Since his arms are fixed and the oars are pivoted, the oars also move backward and forward, and he seems to be rowing. My only hesitation about buying one of these toys for my grandson is that the rower looks rather grim, like a grumpy gondolier.

John Thomas Milson Hircock, an engineer in Birmingham, had higher ambitions in designing his new rocking horse, for he claimed it would be 'very useful in teaching children and young people to attain a firm seat and also as affording considerable exercise for the body whether as a rocking horse in a room or as a galloping horse on ordinary roads or in larger buildings affording sufficient space for turning corners. His claim continues:

> **The simplest form is that of the rocking horse which consists of a single action. In this form the horse itself is fitted underneath ... with a pivot plate ... The horse is then mounted on a cross bar which is carried by a frame ... Across the two front legs of the frame a cross shaft is mounted in bearings with a crank and pedal at each end in such a position as to enable the rider to work the pedals when sitting comfortably on the horse ...**

The pedal shaft is connected via an eccentric and a shaft to the front of the horse, so that 'when the pedal is worked by the rider motion is transferred to it ... which rocks the horse thus imitating the action of a horse'.

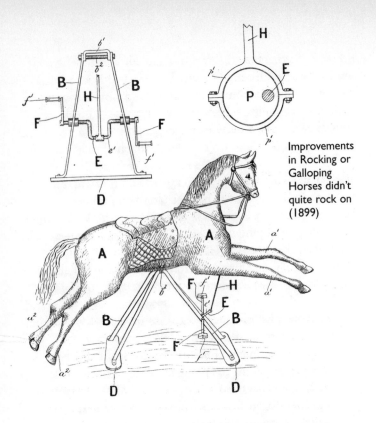

Improvements in Rocking or Galloping Horses didn't quite rock on (1899)

This sounds simple, and looks reasonable in his diagram, but I wonder just how comfortable it would be to work those pedals. Horses are wide, and when you sit on one your knees are pushed well apart; the riding position is quite different from that of a cyclist. I suspect that, if the rocking horse were as wide as, say, a skinny pony, pedalling would be difficult even if it remained stationary, but in fact it would rock up and down, continually taking your feet off the pedals. However, this consideration did not stop Mr Hircock, who went on to make it a real mover.

'To add forward action to the horse the frame is mounted upon wheels ... Then upon the pedal shaft a large sprocket wheel is fixed and a smaller one on the driving shaft which are coupled by a chain …' The rider has reins to control the steering wheel, and is able to speed along the road with a rocking or galloping action. Perhaps this would be fun, but it sounds to me like a rather dangerous form of bicycle!

Golfing gizmos

I had not realised that the passion for golf is at least a hundred years old, since golfing gadgets feature frequently in the patent files of the nineteenth century. A relatively simple, adjustable, skidding golf tee was dreamed up by Agnes Donnelly and Grace Dods of Dumbarton and Jane Ballantyne and John Ballantyne Small of Glasgow, who wanted:

> **to lessen, in some degree, the many difficulties now experienced in shooting the ball from its resting place to destination point. Hitherto, much skill has been required for the purpose of shooting the ball, and, as a consequence, exact or skilful play has been confined to the few select or skilful players of a club. With the use of our adjustable golf tee, greater ease and more exactitude is given to the play and thus the game of golf is rendered still more popular by reason of this ease and exactitude, as aforestated.**

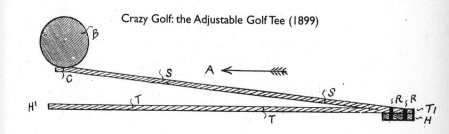

Crazy Golf: the Adjustable Golf Tee (1899)

By means of our improved golf tee, with the ball poised in position and adjusted to the required height from the ground and the skid or skidding arm adjusted to the required angle and the whole spiked firmly to the ground, the player is, thereby, more easily enabled to drive the ball with greater force and with surer aim than has, hitherto, been the rule.

The idea is straightforward: you line up the springy steel tee along the direction in which you want to hit the ball, put the ball in the little cup at the top, and then wallop it with your club, using the sloping arm of the tee as a guide to bring your club head up to the ball at just the right height and at just the right angle.

There seem to me to be two drawbacks to this otherwise clever piece of apparatus. First, the patentees complain that 'exact or skilful play has been confined to the few select or skilful players of a club', but this seems to me to be a good thing. If ever anyone could invent apparatus that enabled all golfers to play with precisely the same skill then the game would become totally boring. Exact play would be tedious in the extreme. Anything that reduces the effect of skill must be bad news; for example, if every player had to fire the ball from a preset catapult on the tee, then presumably every ball would end up in almost the same place on the fairway.

Second, their sliding slope seems to be designed to get the club head both angled upward and moving upward at the moment when it hits the ball. These inventors cannot have come across the work of P.G.Tait, a scientist and a lifelong member of the Royal and Ancient Club at St Andrews, and known to his fellow members as 'the Professor'. After much observation, calculation, and testing he concluded that the well-struck golf ball is enabled to fly as far as it does because it has back-spin; the angled face of all clubs sends the ball off spinning backward up to 50 times a second, and this back-spin coupled with its forward motion gives the ball lift; without this lift the ball would travel only about half as far in the air.

Tait showed that the longest drives leave the ground at an angle of about 8 degrees, and that in order to achieve this the club head must be travelling horizontally when it hits the ball. A club head sliding up this new improved golf tee, whose ramp is at about 7 degrees, would dispatch the ball into the air at roughly 15 degrees, which would make for drives that went very high, but not very far. I think I'll stick with old-fashioned tees.

A dental surgeon in Surrey, Frederick Adolphus Bellamy, invented a game of parlour golf, to be played on a table. Each player was to have a 'club' consisting of a spoon or

Save it for a rainy day: appliances for the Game of Parlour Golf (1899)

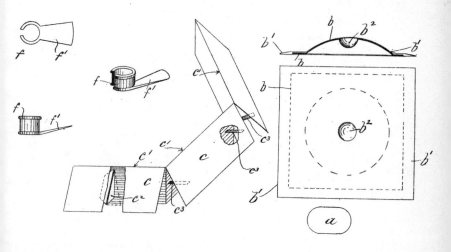

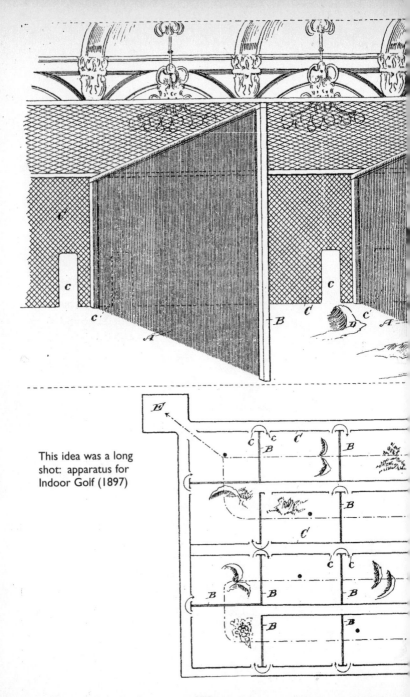

This idea was a long
shot: apparatus for
Indoor Golf (1897)

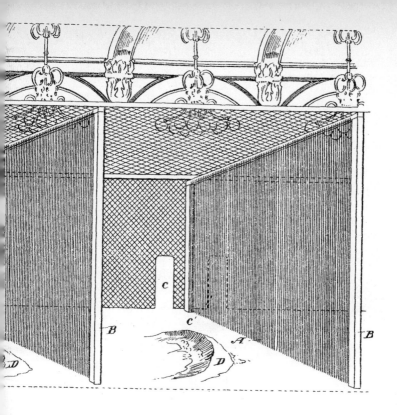

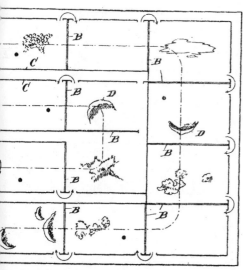

hook attached to a clip or ring fitting on the finger. When used for lofting – to get out of a bunker, for example – the hook faces forward, while for putting it is reversed.

The 'green' and 'hole' are made from a metal plate covered with a cloth which extends beyond the edges of the plate to lie on the table. The plate is dished so that it rises from its edges towards the centre, where there is a depression forming the 'hole'. Irregularities may be formed in the cloth or the plate to imitate rough ground. The 'bunkers' are made from sheets of cardboard folded into V-shapes and secured by hooks or wedges. In his diagram, f is the club, c is a bunker, b^2 is the hole, and a is the tee, made from an extra piece of cloth.

William Harley White of Edinburgh was a printer and publisher of *The Golfer*, and he invented a game of 'short golf' for those who were desperate to have their own course but lacked the rolling acres needed for a conventional course. He said the game could be played 'in restricted areas of ground, roofed or unroofed' – in other words, you could play indoors!

'The apparatus consists of pendant strips or tapes of hemp, cotton, wool, or other spun or woven material, or strips of leather, rubber, or other material set up to partially impede the progress of a golf ball when driven against it …' These pendant strips were to be hung from bars and to reach the ground. The ball was to be played 'from in front of the apparatus with a full stroke, as on open ground. The ball in striking against the pendant strings or strips is partially retarded in its motion, the amount of retardation being arranged by the number of lines of strings or strips it has to pass through before reaching the other side of the apparatus.'

He suggested that there should be nine or eighteen holes, with at least three strokes for each hole, each one needing its own array of hanging strips:

First, drive off tee through apparatus. Second, drive through green through apparatus. Third, approach to putting green through apparatus. ... Hazards and bunkers can be placed about the ground between each apparatus ...

The line of the course can be confined by netting or other dividing material, and players can pass through the apparatus by pushing the strings or strips aside ... The putting greens can be of turf, rubber, cloth, cork, linoleum or other suitable material. The strings or strips of apparatus may be more sparsely distributed in direct line of drive through, so as to allow the straight driving player an advantage of getting his ball through easier than a badly driven ball.

In principle it sounds as though this game could be playable, but I am amazed at the scale of the operation. A course of 27 holes would require hundreds of yards of hanging strips, and hundreds of yards of scaffolding to hang them on, which would be enormously expensive. However, the space would be an even greater problem. In order to be able to play 'a full stroke' you need a minimum space of something like four yards (3.6 metres) square, otherwise you would always be hitting the apparatus with your club. White claims that nine holes of (at least) three strokes each could be fitted into a third of an acre, which is about the area of a tennis court. What's more, in his sketch of the apparatus (see over) he shows it set up inside what appears to be a great hall or conservatory. I don't know many people who have halls or conservatories covering a third of an acre, and I imagine that people who actually own such huge rooms might well have enough space in the grounds to lay out a real golf course.

Musical mayhem

Lacking television or even radio, Victorian families were forced to entertain themselves in the evenings, and music making was a popular pastime. Young ladies were encouraged to play the piano, and a problem that must have beset most households was how to turn the pages of the music without a helpful sister standing patiently by your shoulder. Henry Benjamin Wing spotted this problem, and patented a simple solution: small metal clips (or gummed tags of stiff paper) to attach to the edge of the page, so that it could easily be flipped over between notes. As he pointed out, 'The clips can be attached one to each leaf at a different point and the ends project so that they can be seized by the tips of the fingers. As there is only one clip for each leaf there is no danger of two leaves being turned accidentally.'

However, this was far too simple for Johann Schweinfurth II and Heinrich Bechdolf, who designed a

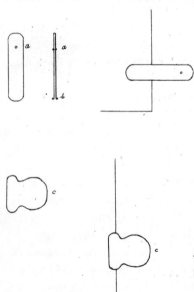

wondrous machine to do the same job. The mechanism is complicated to explain, but should have been simple to operate, since pressing a foot pedal once would turn one page, pressing again would turn the next, and so on. In fact this looks to me like a slightly advanced version of the machine

This invention was in the wrong key: the means for Turning the Leaves of Music (1899)

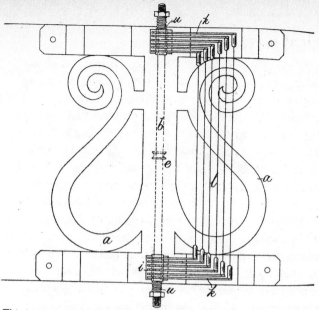

This invention was obviously missing the key to success: the Appliance for Turning Over Music defies explanation (1899)

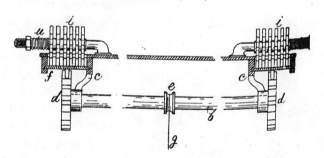

invented by Augustin Lajarrige in 1887, which turned the pages of music at the nudge of the pianist's knee. If I were a pianist, I'd like to have one of these – and yet I have never seen a pianist use anything like it.

In 1881 Benjamin Atkins of Cincinnati, Ohio, produced a painful-looking device intended to hold the pianist's fingers horizontal, as far as the second joint. This, he claimed,

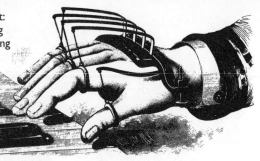

Suffering for your art: this finger-supporting device for this budding pianist looks like torture — small wonder no one wanted to play along! (1899)

would improve the player's touch and allow more rapid fingering, although it looks to me as though this chunk of machinery would slow you down and rapidly make your arms tired.

Finally, not content with the normal musical instruments at their disposal, enterprising musicians have invented dozens more, with varying degrees of complexity and success. In 1895 Professor Bruno Wollenhaupt of New York made a new violin with 12 extra strings inside, covering an octave in semitones. These were intended to resonate with

the normal strings, greatly enriching the tone and volume of the instrument (although many parents find normal violins quite loud enough!), and could be damped by the violinist with a slight movement of the chin.

One-man band: the combined cello-piano and viola-piano were not bound for musical stardom (1893)

In 1893 a cello teacher, Mr de Vlaminck, depressed by his students' incompetence at getting accurate pitch with their left hands, produced a combination cello-piano, in which the left hand plays a keyboard, which frets the strings precisely, while the right hand bows the strings in the usual way. He claimed that the usual effects could be obtained with the bow, and the keyboard provides the accuracy of tone which has been set once and for all. The keys are so perfectly linked to the hammers resting on the strings that it is even possible to produce the slight tremolo associated with playing with feeling!

Meanwhile, in London, John Matthias Augustus Stroh invented an entirely new instrument, in which the body of a violin with its sounding board was replaced by a frame attached to a drumhead fitted with a trumpet-shaped resonance tube. There is a direct connection between the violin bridge and the diaphragm, so that vibrations from the strings are passed directly to the diaphragm, and its resonance is amplified by the tube. I find it hard to imagine what this would have sounded like.

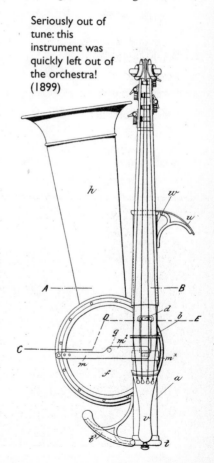

Seriously out of tune: this instrument was quickly left out of the orchestra! (1899)

Further reading

Brown, G. I., *The Guinness History of Inventions*, Guinness 1996

Clarke, Donald (ed), *The Encyclopedia of Inventions*, Marshall Cavendish 1977

Derry, T. K. & Williams, Trevor I., *A Short History of Technology,* Oxford UP 1960, Dover 1993

de Vries, Leonard, *Victorian Inventions,* John Murray 1971

Harris, Melvin, *The ITN Book of Firsts*, Michael O'Mara 1994

Hart-Davis, Adam & Bader, Paul, *The Local Heroes Book of British Ingenuity,* Sutton 1997

Hart-Davis, Adam & Bader, Paul, *More Local Heroes*, Sutton 1998

Hart-Davis, Adam, *Thunder, Flush, and Thomas Crapper,* Michael O'Mara 1997

Robertson, Patrick, *The Shell Book of Firsts*, Ebury Press & Michael Joseph 1974

Tibbals, Geoff, *The Guinness Book of Innovations*, Guinness 1994

On the subject of perpetual motion, there is a mass of material both in *Encyclopaedia Britannica* 9th edn, 1885, and on the Internet. For inventions in detail nothing can beat the original patents, which can be consulted at the old Patent Office in London, or in various other places around the country.

Picture Acknowledgements

JOLYON TROSCIANKO: 11, 56, 76, 78, 79, 80, 100, 102

THE PATENT OFFICE: 6, 10, 14, 23, 44, 66, 74, 95, 97, 99, 103, 108, 111, 122, 126, 138, 141, 142, 143, 144, 152, 158, 161, 162, 164, 166, 167, 169, 170, 174, 175, 177

SCIENTIFIC AMERICAN: 2, 3, 13, 22, 38, 42, 47, 52, 57, 58, 88, 93, 98, 129, 145, 155, 176, 177

LA NATURE: 139, 159

DE NATUUR: 1, 49, 53, 75, 149

BRISTOL MUSEUMS & ART GALLERY: 153, 154

ENGINEERS & MECHANICS ENCYCLOPEDIA 1836: 30

DOVER IMAGES: 87, 107, 111

All other pictures were provided by the author.

Index